Guitar/Vocal

CLASSIC

EAGLES

Authentic
GUITAR-TAB
Edition
Includes Complete Solos

W9-ADF-293

Transcribed and Arranged by *HEMME B. LUTTJEBOER*

"Eagles On The Border" Album Cover Painting: Beatian Yazz;
© 1974 Elektra/Asylum Records

"Hotel California"
© 1976 Elektra/Asylum/Nonesuch Records

"One Of These Nights" Album Photo by Tom Kelley Studios
Artpiece & Lettering by Boyd Elder

"Desperado" Album Photography & Lettering: Henry Diltz
© 1973 Elektra/Asylum Records for the United States
and WEA International, Inc. for the world outside of the United States

"Eagles" Album Photography: Henry Diltz
© 1972 Elektra/Asylum Records for the United States
and WEA International, Inc. for the world outside of the United States

CONTENTS

Key To Notation Symbols

ALREADY GONE

Words and Music by
JACK TEMPCHIN and ROBB STRANDLUND

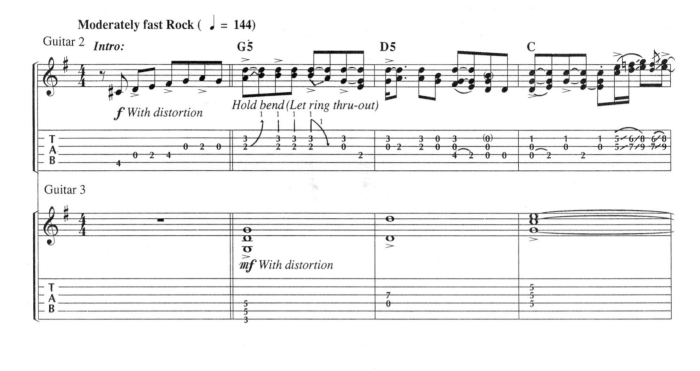

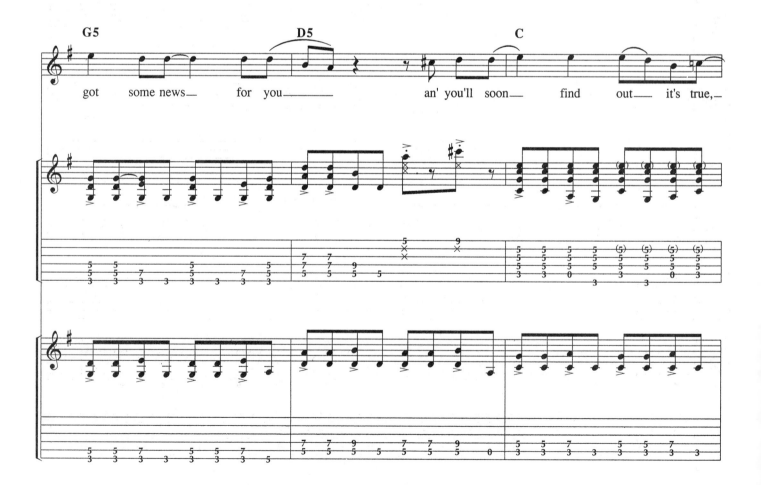

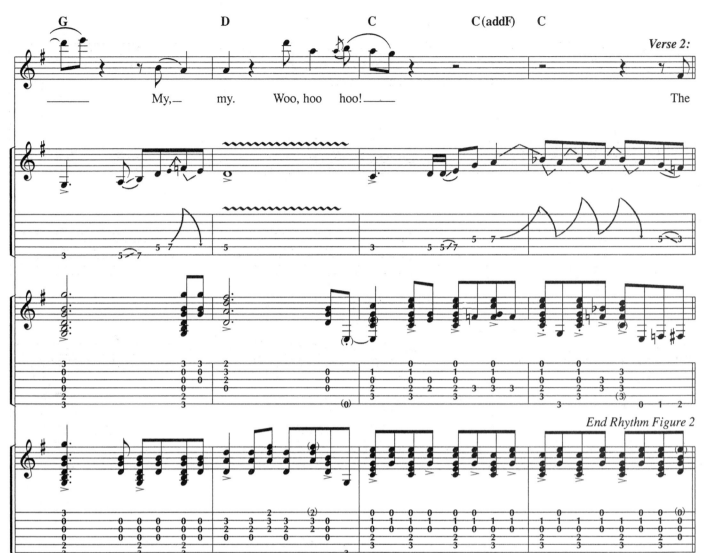

Verse 2:

My,— my. Woo, hoo hoo!—

The

End Rhythm Figure 2

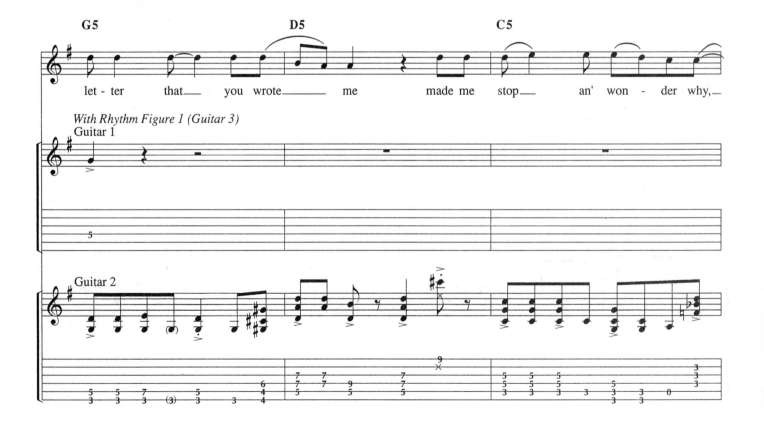

let - ter that— you wrote— me made me stop— an' won - der why,—

With Rhythm Figure 1 (Guitar 3)
Guitar 1

Guitar 2

look up___ in___ the sky___ you can see___ the stars___ an' still___

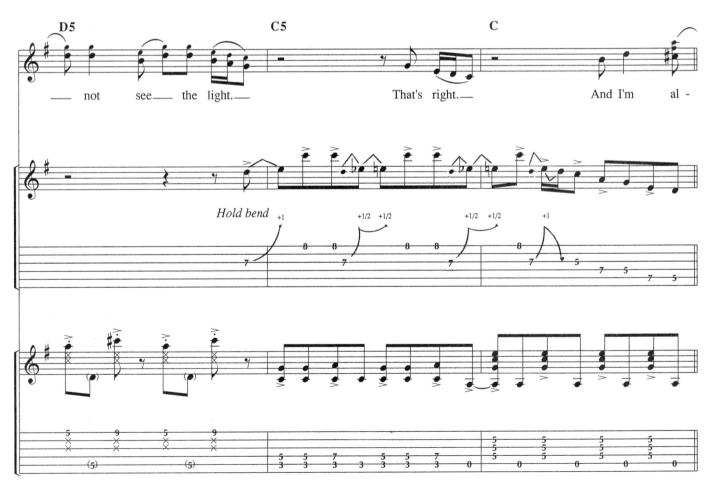

___ not see___ the light.___ That's right.___ And I'm al -

strong,—   I will   sing——————————

— this   vic - t'ry song,——————   woo,——— hoo!—

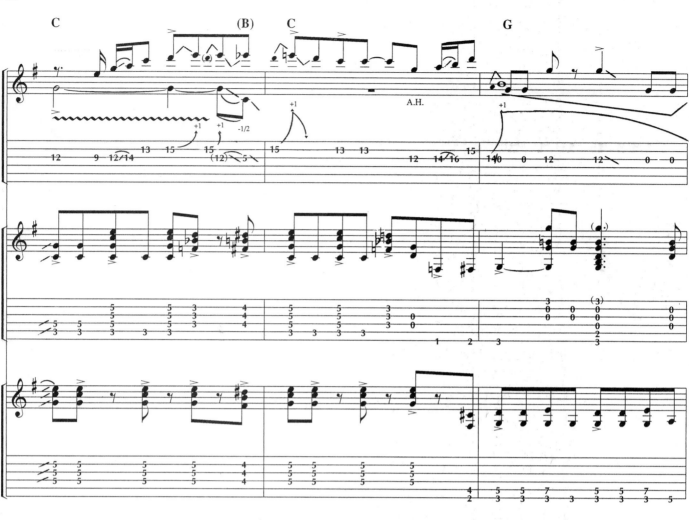

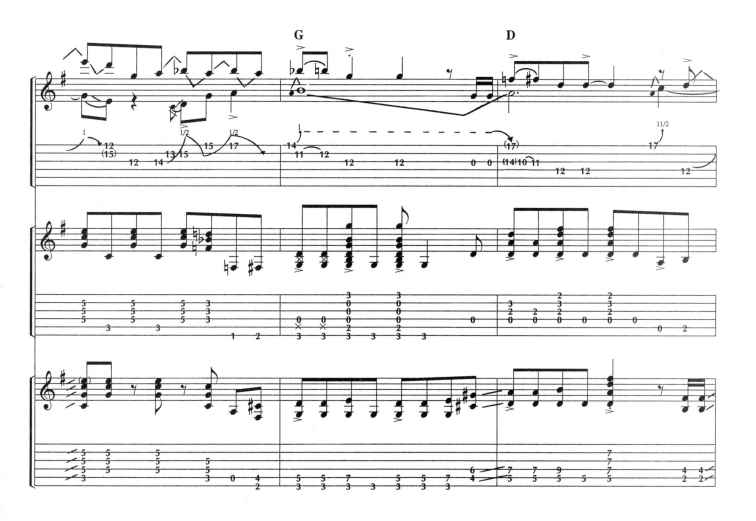

18

knows_ it was - n't you_ who set me free._
Oo.

So_ of - ten - times_ it hap - pens that we
Oo.

live our lives in chains___ an' we nev-er e - ven know___

Oo.___

we have___ the key.___

But me, I'm al -

22

strong,— I will sing (I will sing)

— this vic - t'ry song.— 'Cause I'm al -

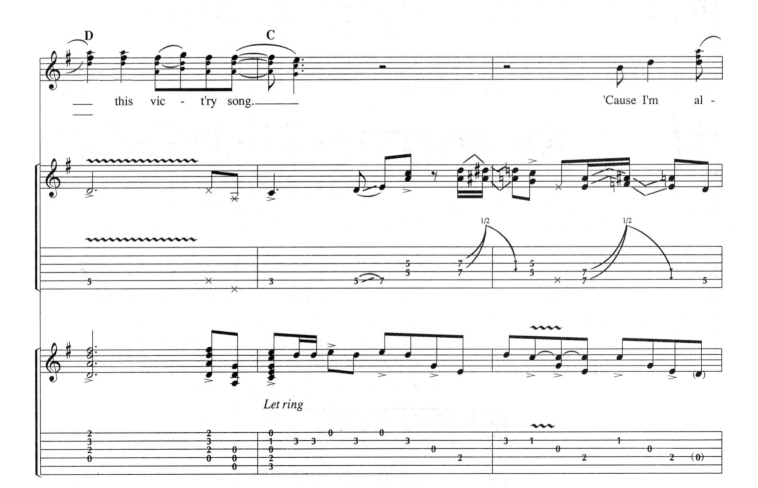

Guitar 3 substitute Rhythm Fill 2

Rhythm Fill 2 - Guitar 3

26

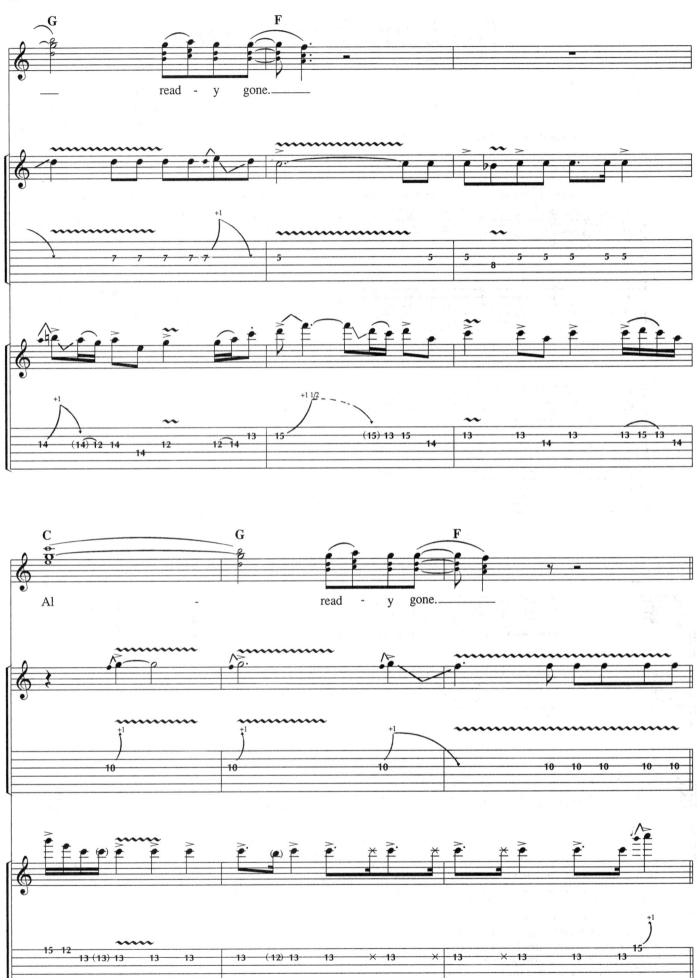

The Best Of My Love

Words and Music by
DON HENLEY, GLENN FREY
and JOHN DAVID SOUTHER

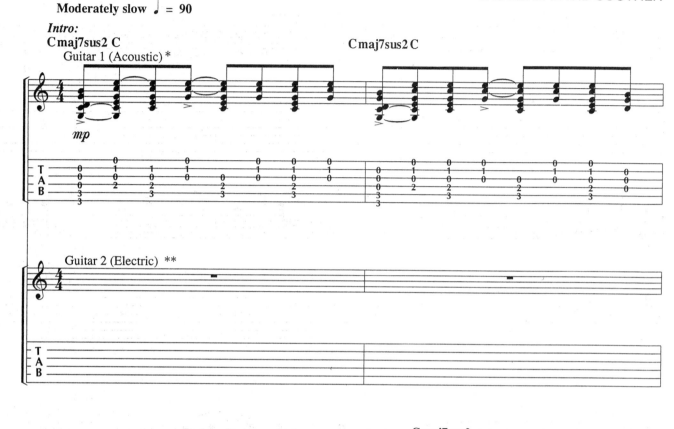

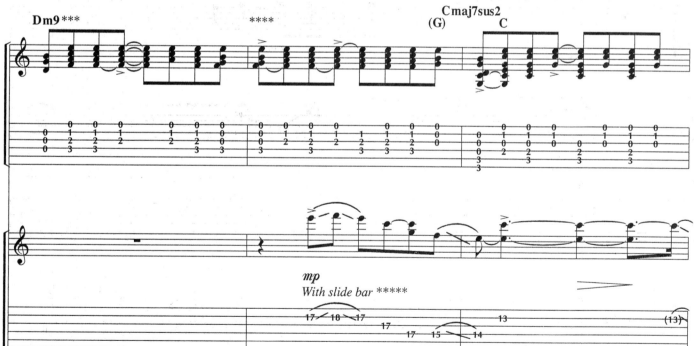

*Doubled by 12 string acoustic capoed at 3rd fret.
**Pedal steel arranged for electric 6 string.
*** Chord harmony determined by bass figure.
****Pedal steel, bass and drums enter.
*****Play all notes with slide where possible.

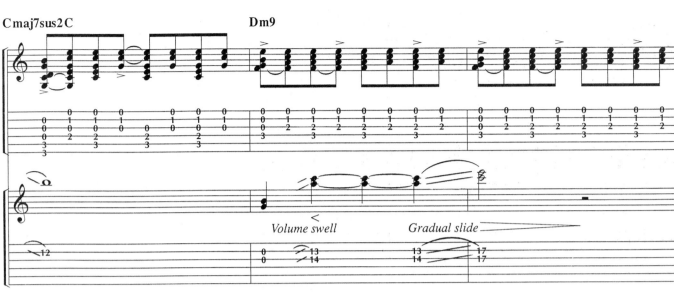

Verse 1:

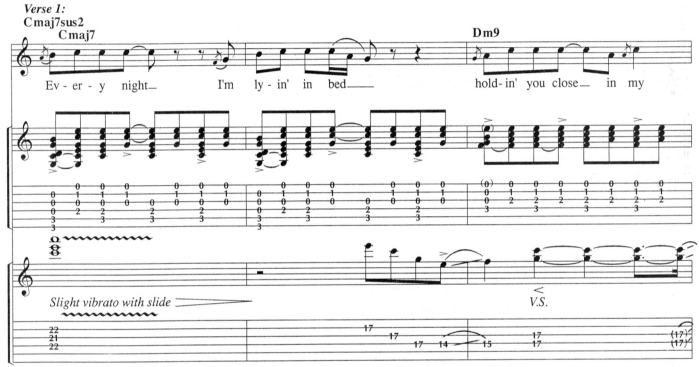

Ev-er-y night___ I'm ly-in' in bed___ hold-in' you close___ in my

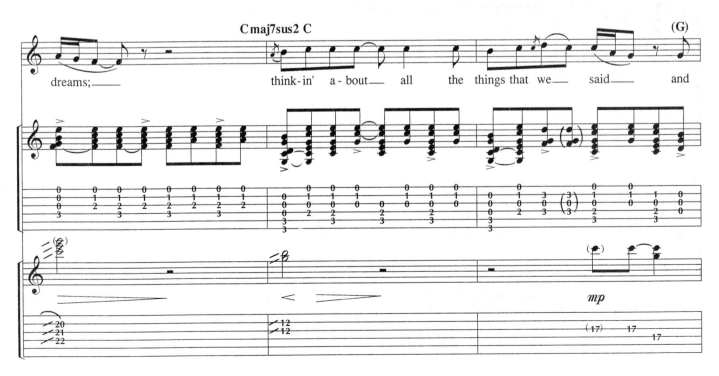

dreams;___ think-in' a-bout___ all the things that we___ said___ and

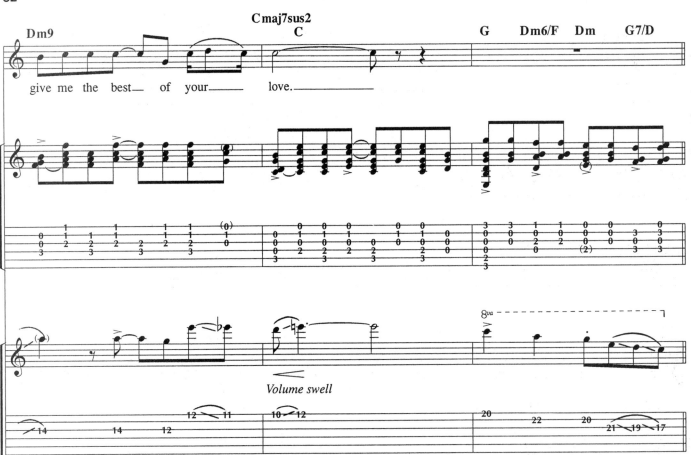

give me the best— of your— love.——————

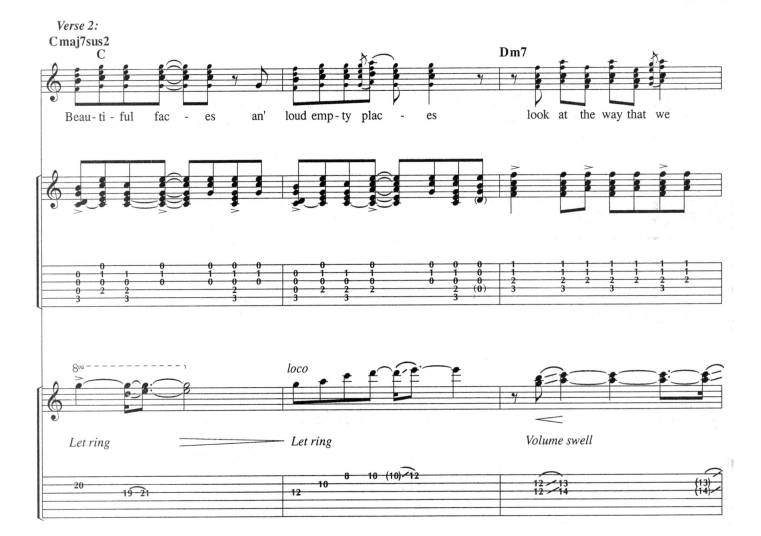

Verse 2:

Beau- ti - ful fac - es an' loud emp- ty plac - es look at the way that we

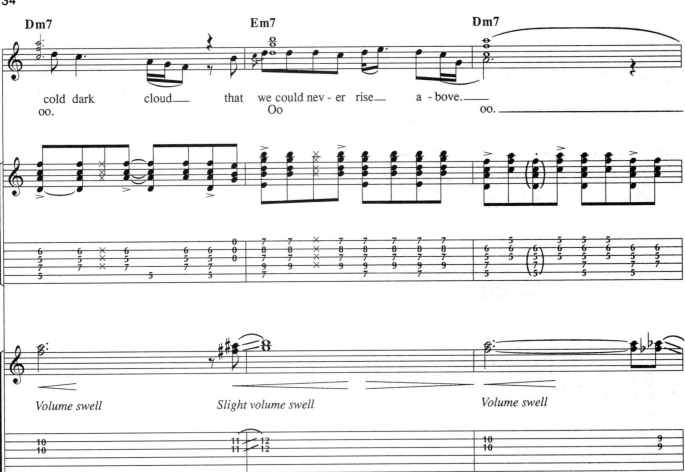

cold dark cloud___ that we could nev-er rise___ a-bove.
oo. Oo oo. _____

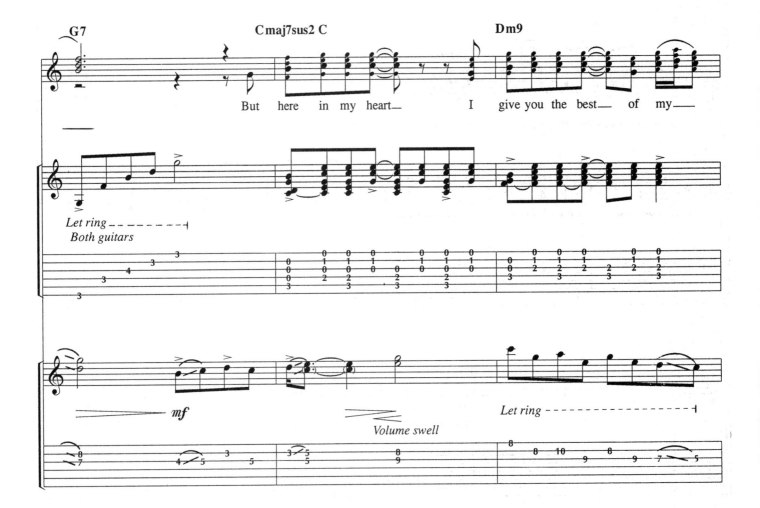

But here in my heart___ I give you the best___ of my___

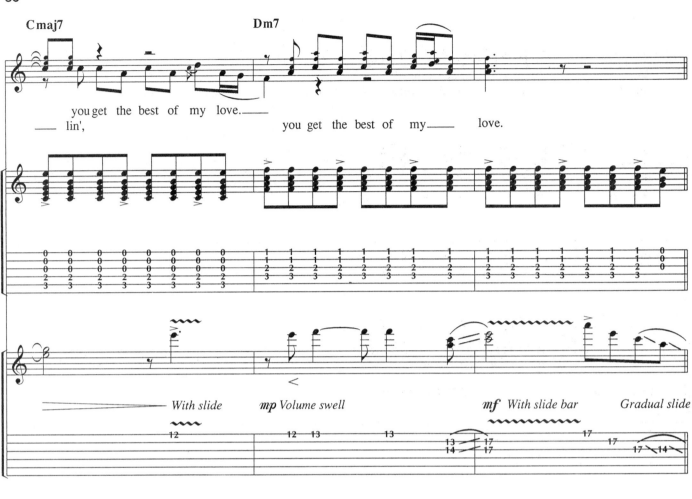

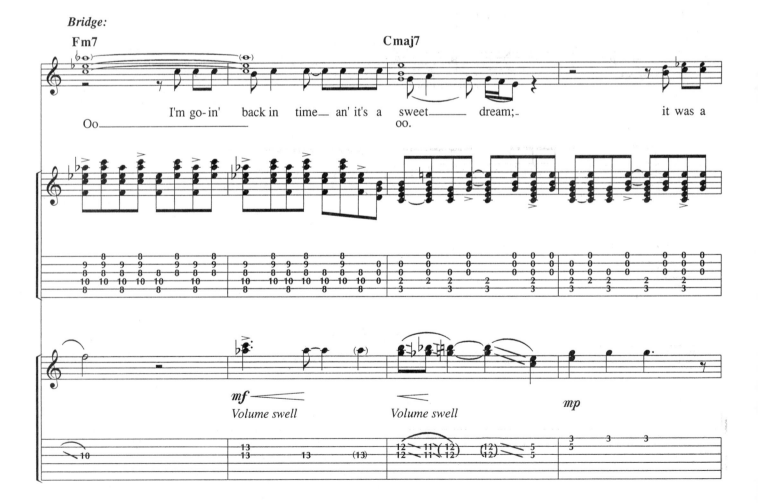

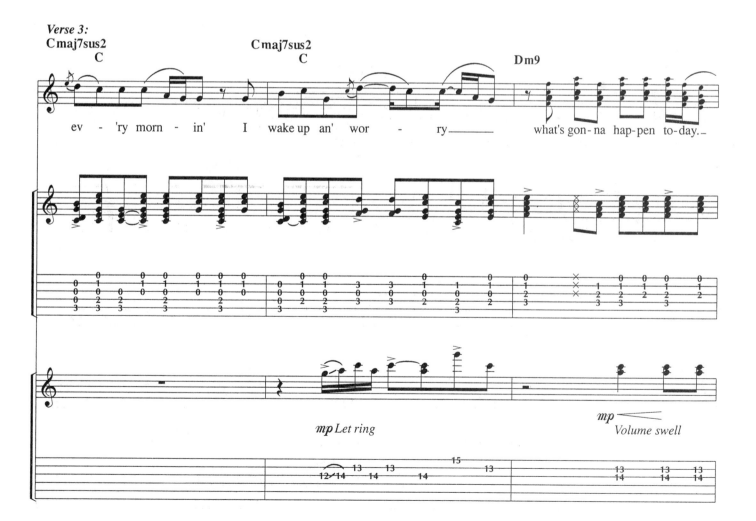

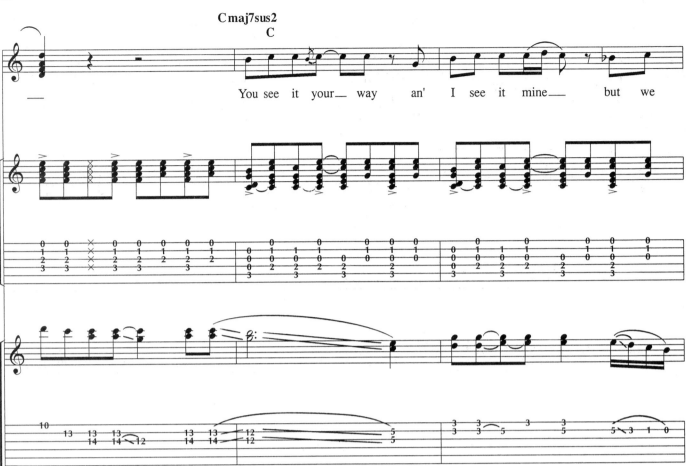

Cmaj7sus2 / C

You see it your way an' I see it mine __ but we

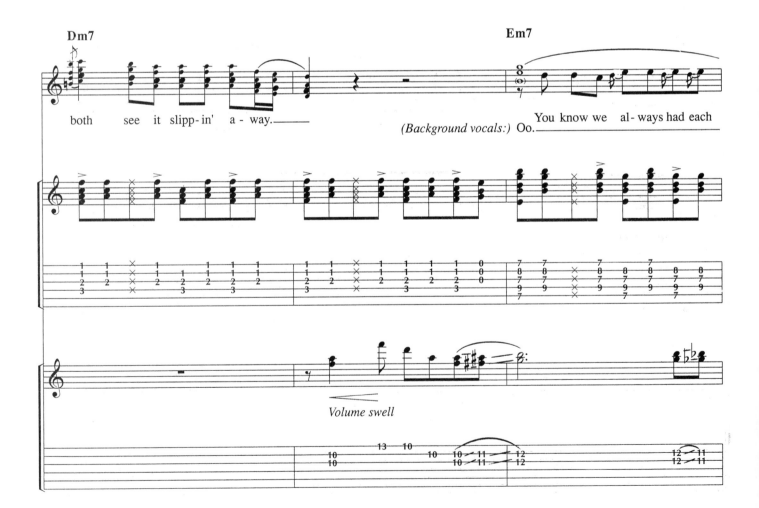

both see it slipp-in' a - way. __

(Background vocals:) Oo. __ You know we al-ways had each

Dm7

Em7

Volume swell

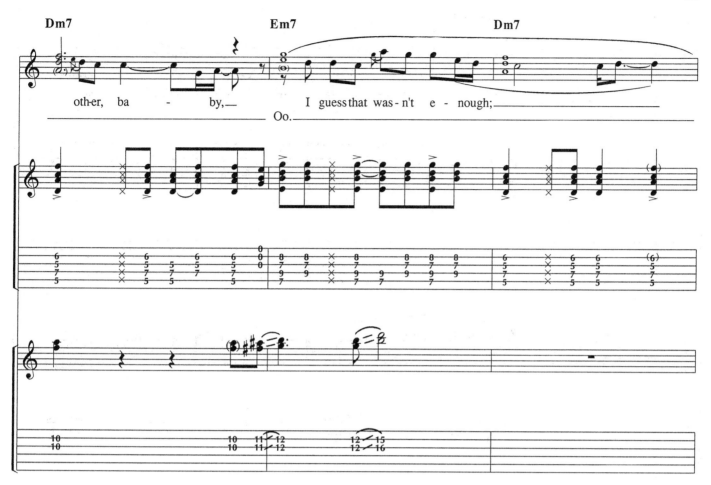

other, ba - by,   I guess that was-n't e - nough;
Oo.

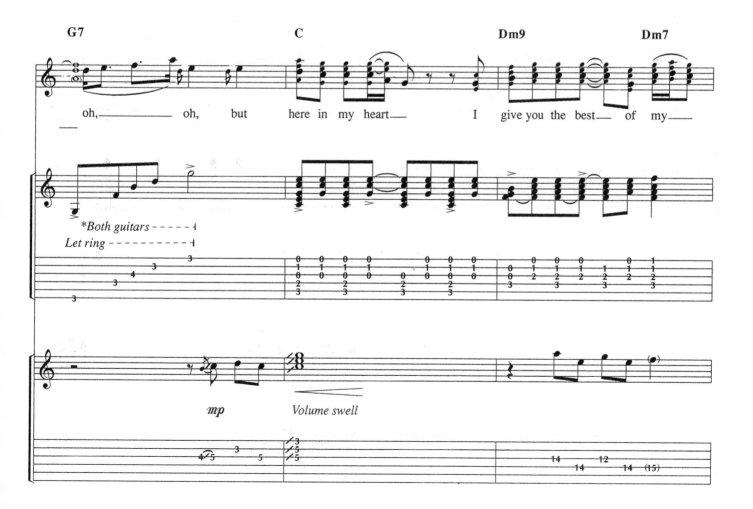

oh,   oh,   but   here in my heart   I   give you the best   of my

*Both guitars
Let ring

mp   Volume swell

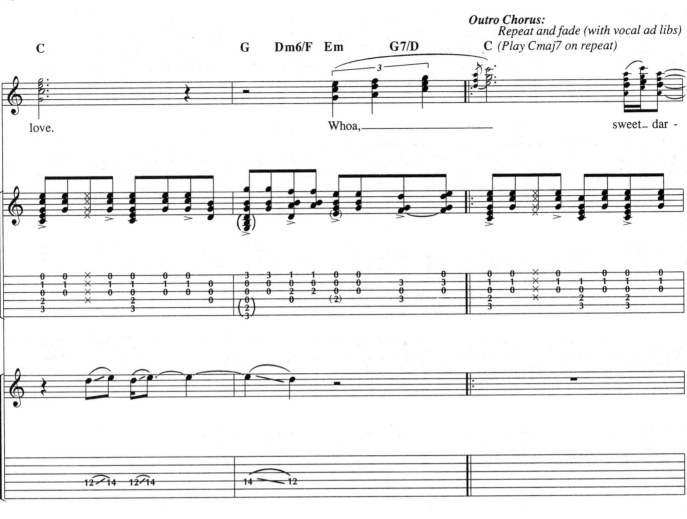

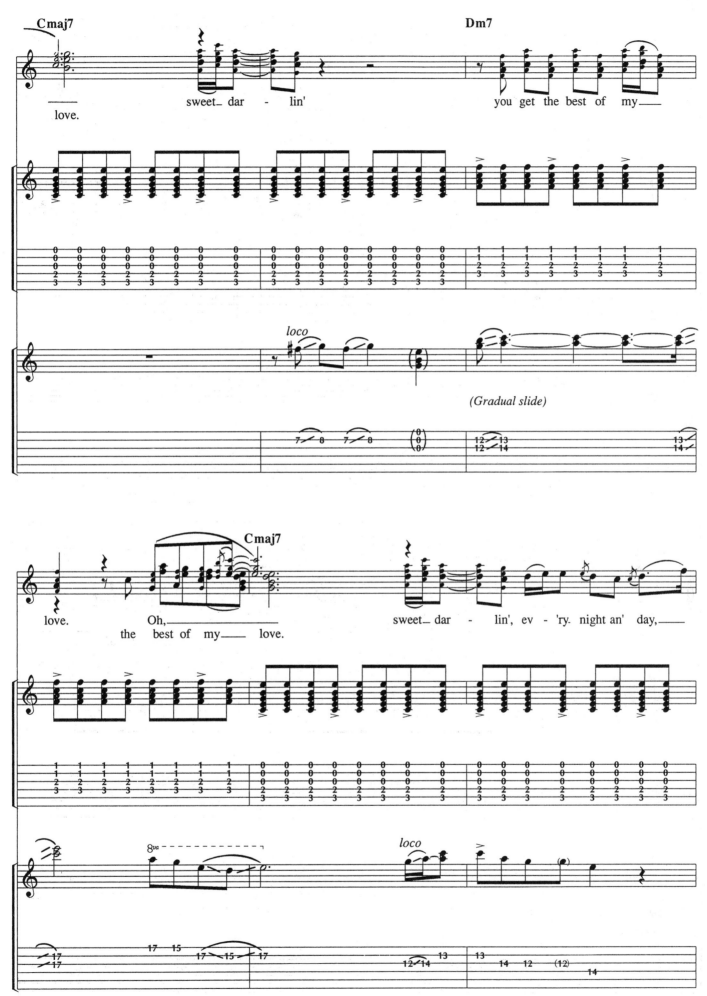

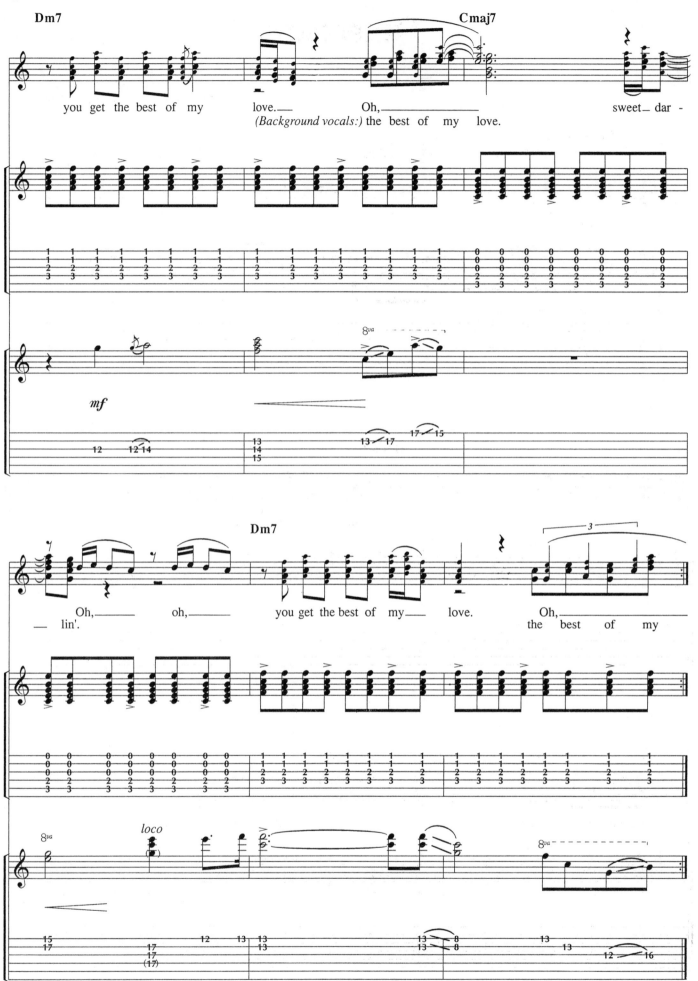

you get the best of my love.___ Oh,_____ sweet_ dar -
(Background vocals:) the best of my love.

Oh,_____ oh,_____ you get the best of my_ love. Oh,_____
_ lin'. the best of my

Desperado

Words and Music by
DON HENLEY and GLENN FREY

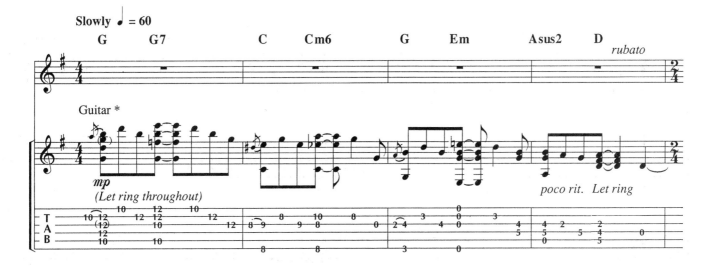

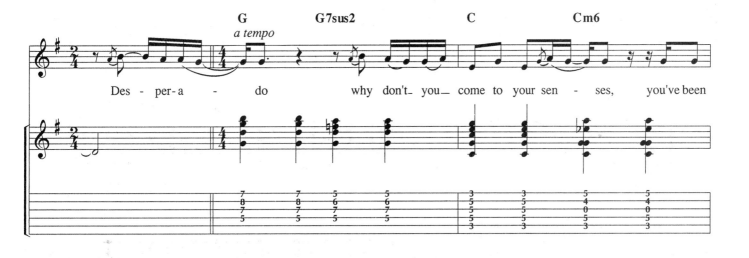

* Piano arranged for Guitar

you got your rea - sons, these things that are pleas - in' you___ can hurt you__some - how.

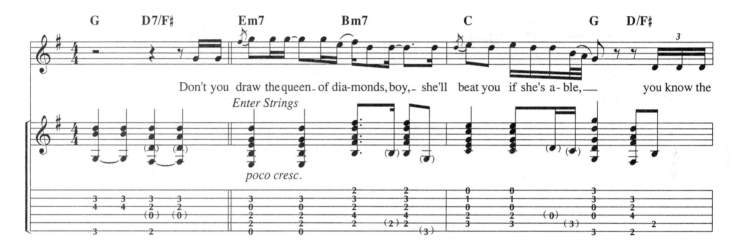

Don't you draw the queen__ of dia-monds, boy,__ she'll beat you if she's a - ble,___ you know the

Enter Strings

poco cresc.

queen of hearts__is al - ways your best bet._____ Now it seems to me__ some fine__ things__ have been

laid up - on__ your ta - ble, but you on - ly want__ the ones___ that you can't get.__

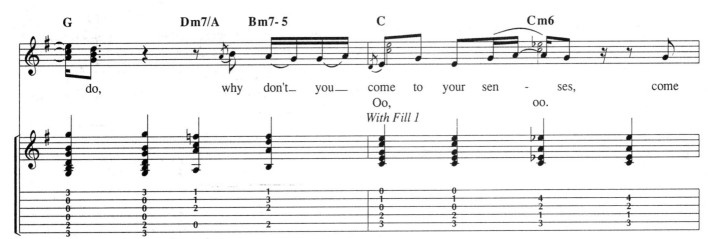

do, why don't you come to your sen - ses, come

With Fill 1

Oo, oo.

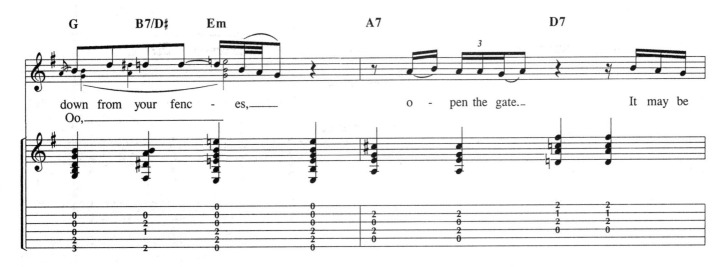

down from your fenc - es, o - pen the gate. It may be

Oo,

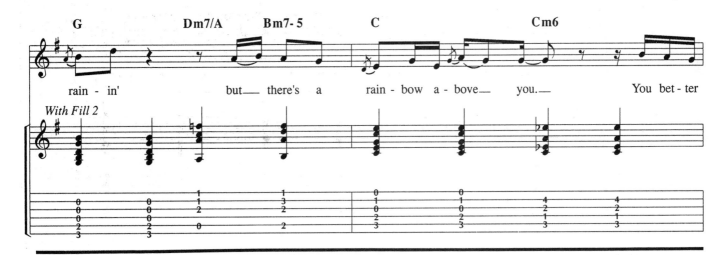

rain - in' but there's a rain - bow a - bove you. You bet - ter

With Fill 2

Fill 1

mp

Clean tone Electric

Fill 2

mp

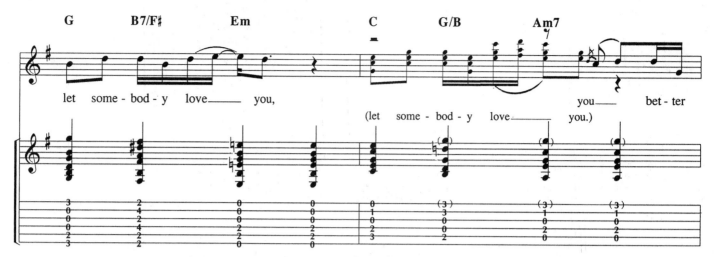

let some - bod - y love____ you, (let some - bod - y love____ you.) you____ bet - ter

let some - bod - y love____ you,____ be - fore it's too_____ late._

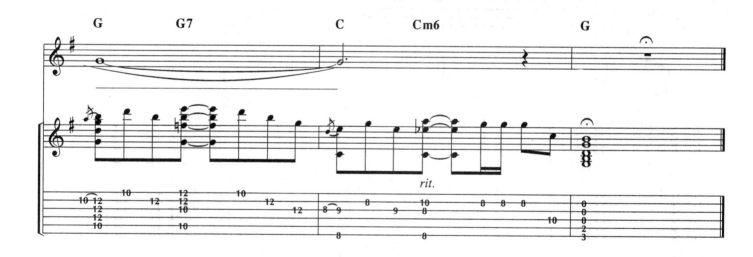

Life In The Fast Lane

Words and Music by
**DON HENLEY, GLENN FREY
and JOE WALSH**

held her for ran - som in the heart_____ of the cold,_ cold_ cit - y.   He had a

nas-ty rep-u-ta-tion as a cru-el   dude,_   they said he was ruth-less,   (they) said he was crude._   They had

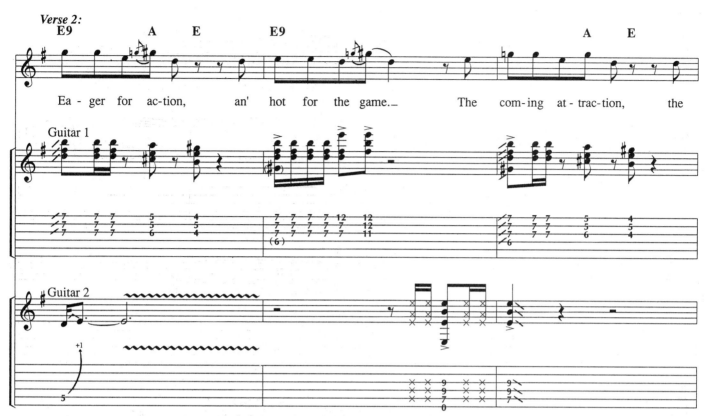

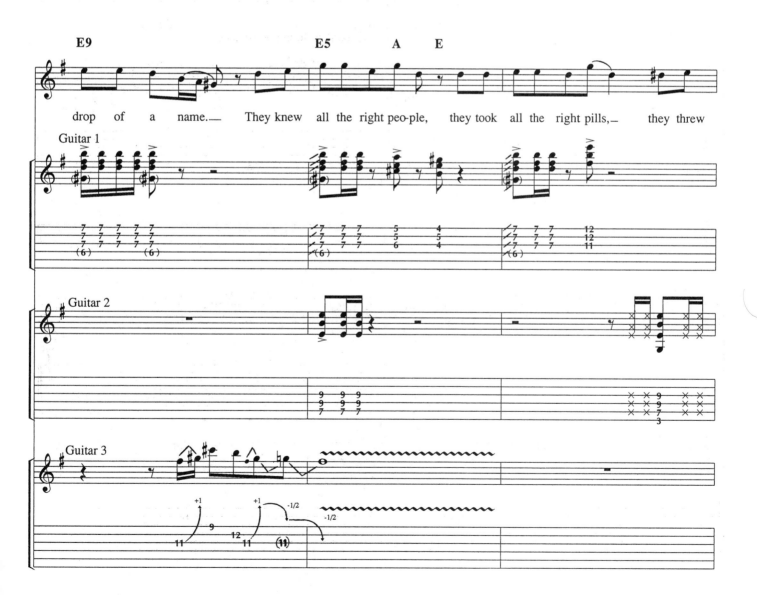

56

Guitar 4 in E tuning: ① = E, ② = B, ③ = G#, ④ = E, ⑤ = B, ⑥ = E

Guitar Solo

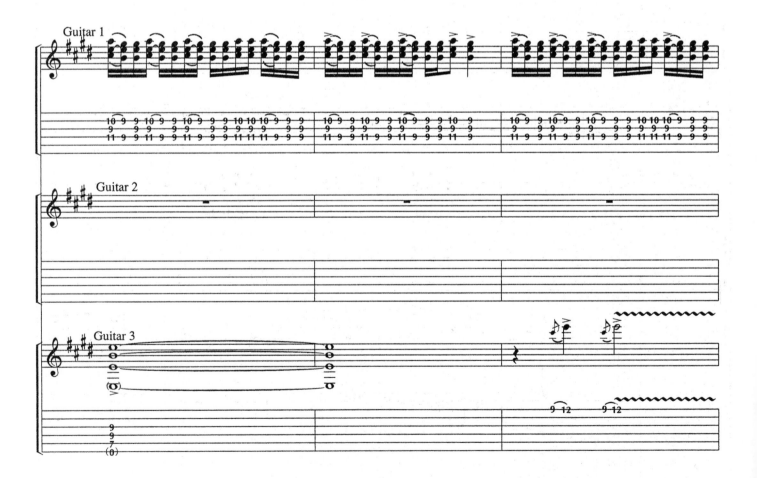

Verse 3:

Blow-in' and burn-in' blind - ed by thirst,— they——— did - n't see the stop sign,— took a turn—

— for the worst.— She said, "lis - ten, ba-by, you can hear the en-gine ring,— we've been

60

Right-hand finger taps

62

Life in the fast—— lane.——

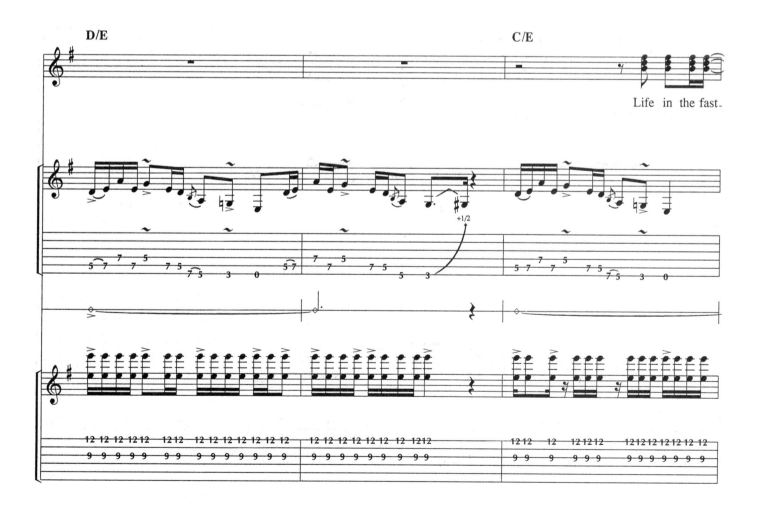

Life in the fast.

A/E

lane.

Outro:
Figure A:

New Kid In Town

Words and Music by
DON HENLEY, GLENN FREY
and JOHN DAVID SOUTHER

Keyboard arranged for guitar.

There's talk on the street— it sounds— so— fa-mil - iar.—

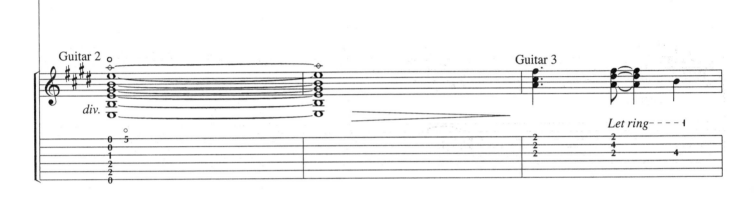

Great ex - pec - ta - tions, ev -'ry-bod-y's

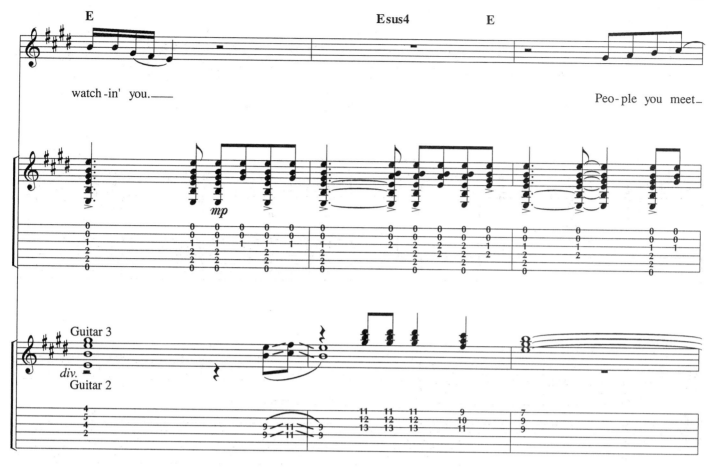

watch-in' you.___   Peo-ple you meet_

— they all_ seem_ to know_ you._   E-ven your old_

_____ friends treat you like you're some-thing new. _____

John-ny come late-ly, the new kid _____ in _____

the new kid— in— town.

Will she still

love— you

Ah.

when you're not a - round?

but night af-ter night you're wil-ling to hold——her, just

hold——her. Tears—— on—— your shoul - der.——

Guitar 2 to left of line on tab./Guitar 3 to right of line on tab.

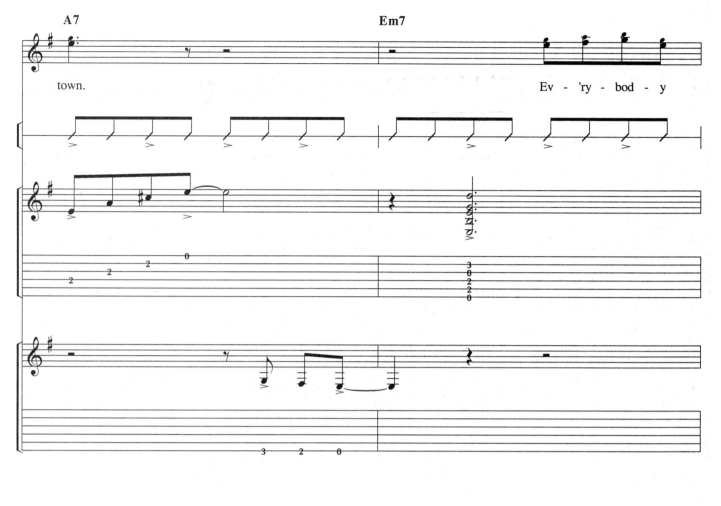

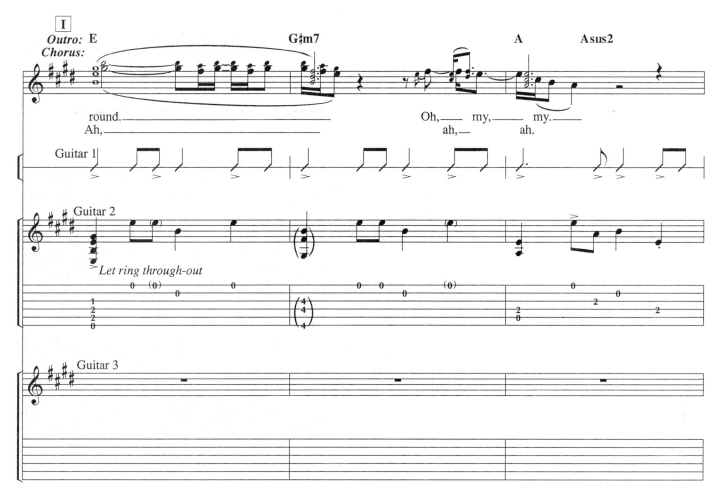

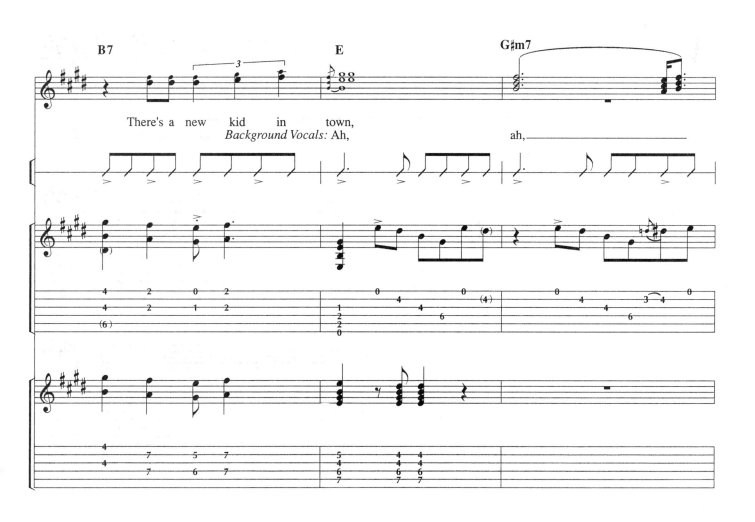

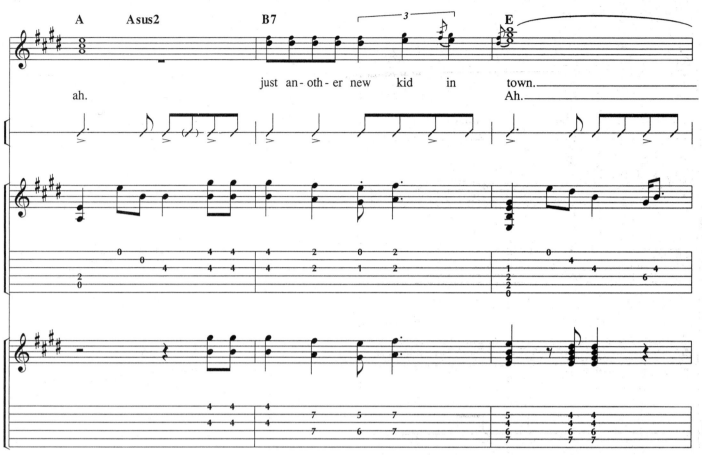

just an-oth-er new kid in town.

ah.

Ah.

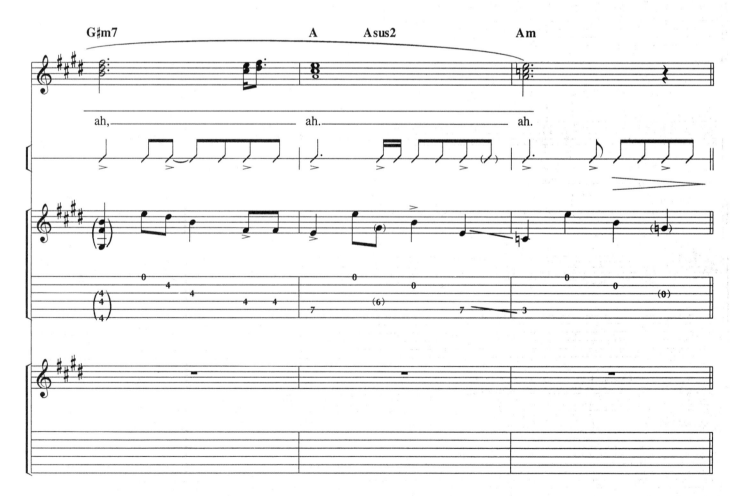

ah,

ah.

ah.

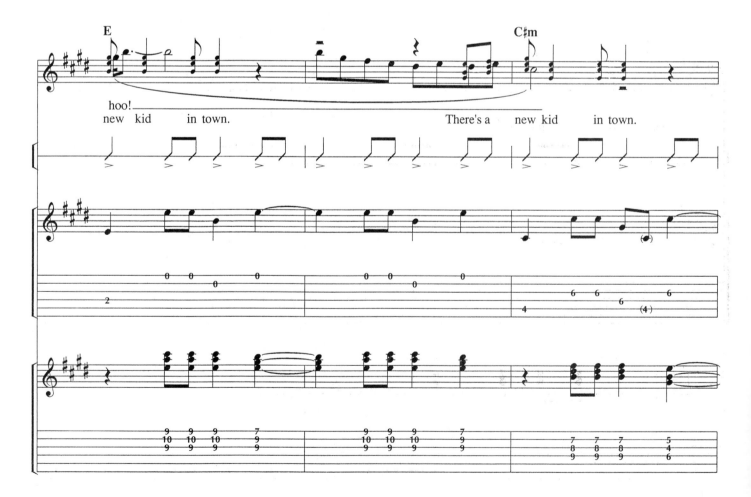

There's a   new kid   in town.   Ev - 'ry - bod - y's talk - in'.   There's a

new kid   in town.   Peo - ple start - ed walk - in'   There's a

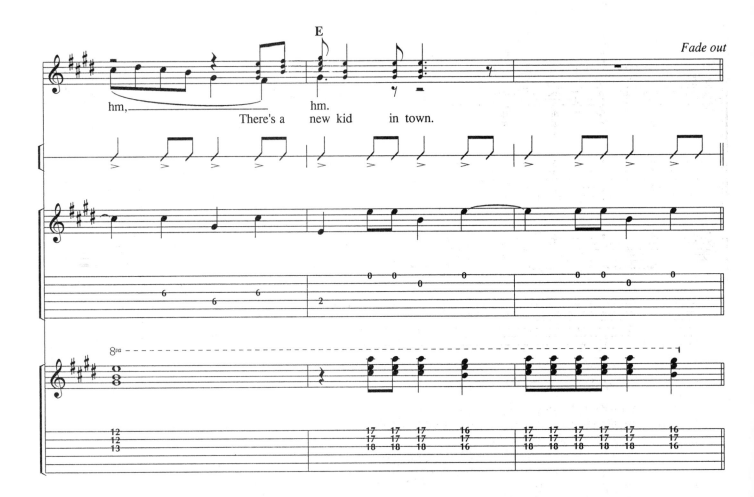

Peaceful Easy Feeling

Words and Music by
JACK TEMPCHIN

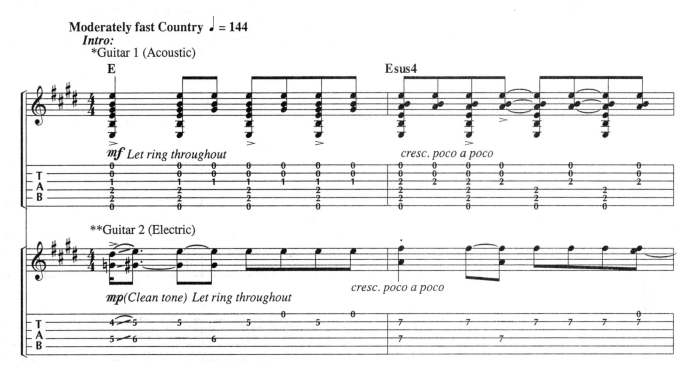

*Doubled by six string acoustic capoed at IV fret.

**Guitar 2 is played with a "Parsons-White" pull-string bender.
   This arrangement is written for standard guitar simulating the device as best as possible. Use light strings!

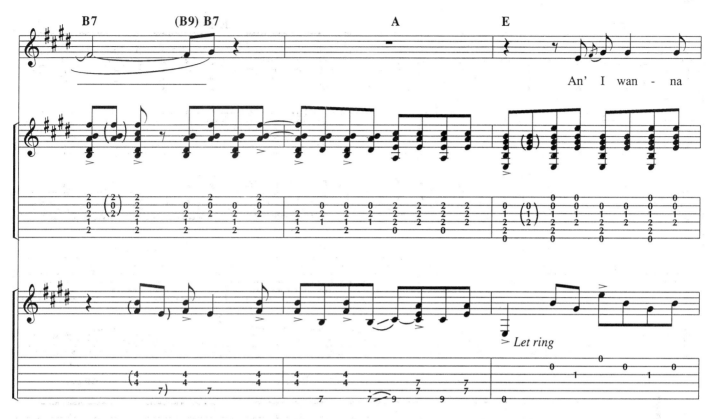

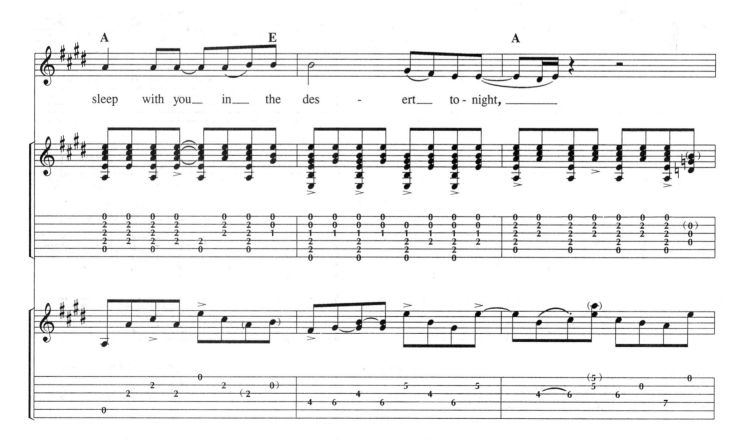

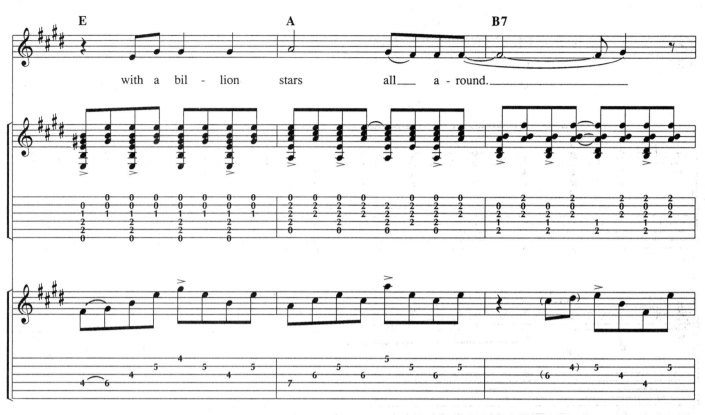

with a bil - lion stars all___ a - round._____

Chorus:

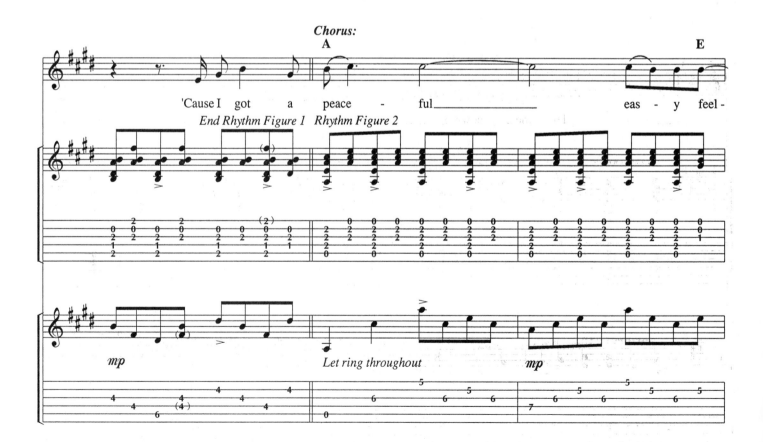

'Cause I got a peace - ful_____ eas - y feel-

End Rhythm Figure 1 Rhythm Figure 2

mp

Let ring throughout

mp

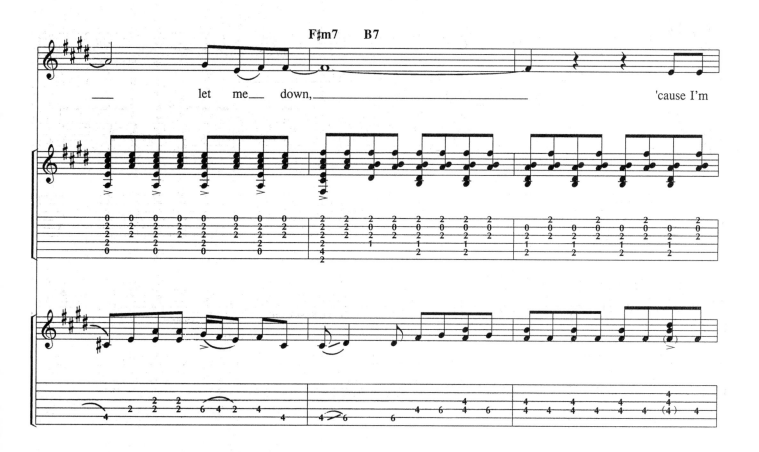

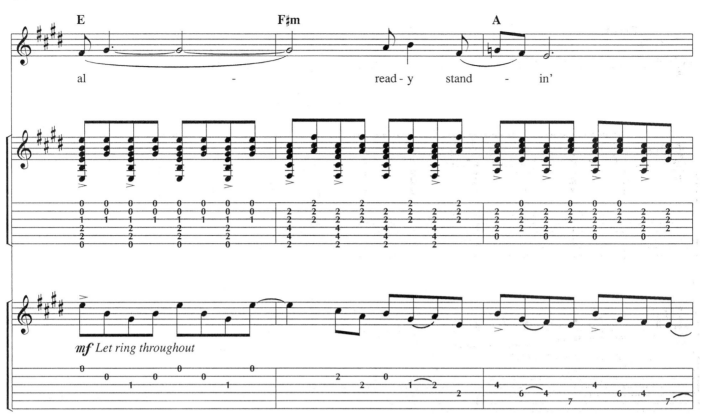

al - read-y stand - in'

mf *Let ring throughout*

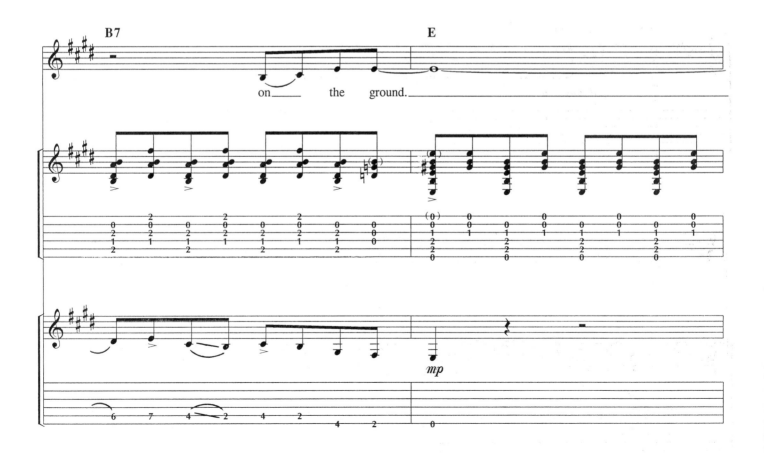

on_____ the ground._____

mp

Guitar Solo
With Rhythm Figures 1 & 2 (simile)

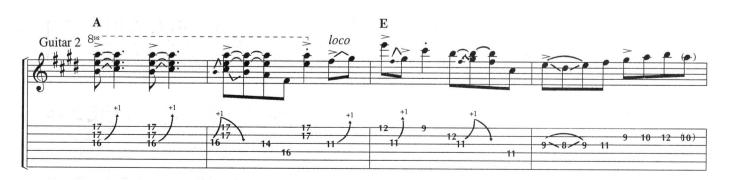

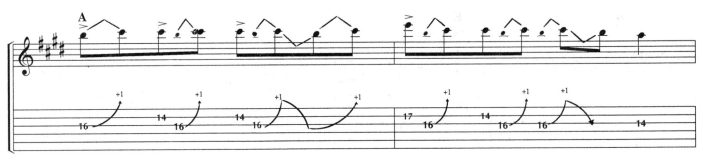

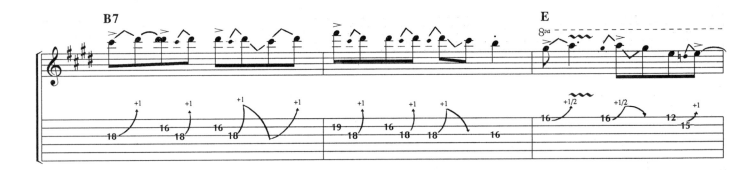

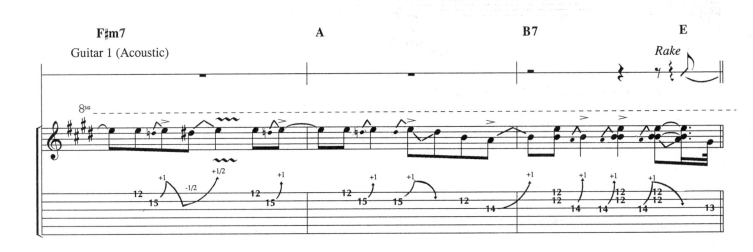

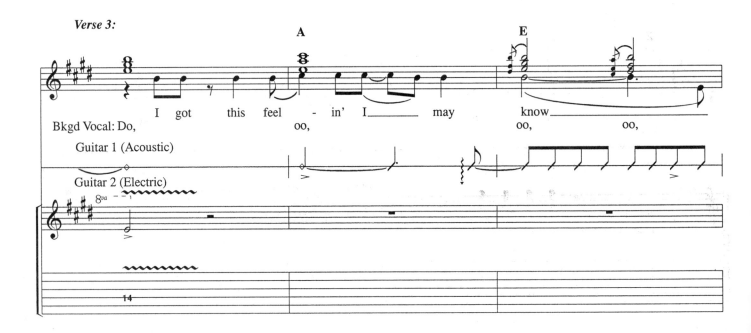

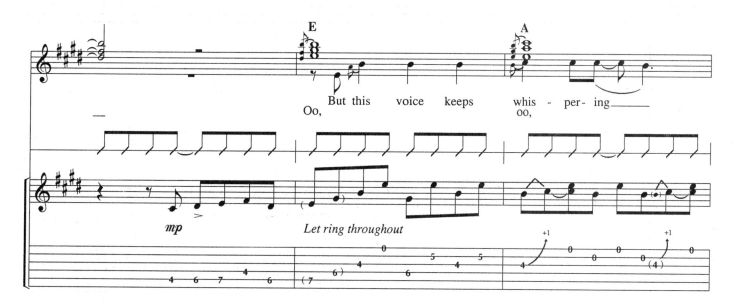

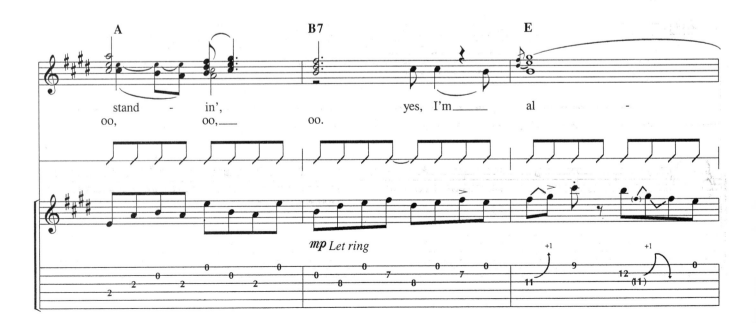

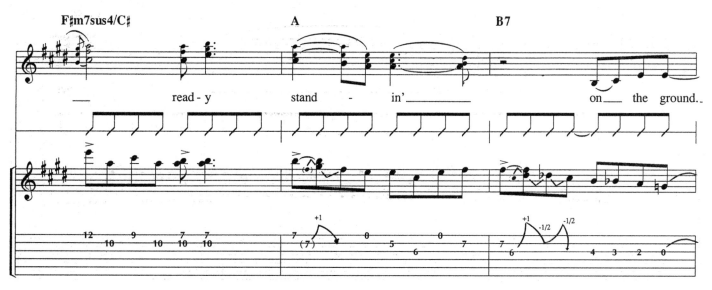

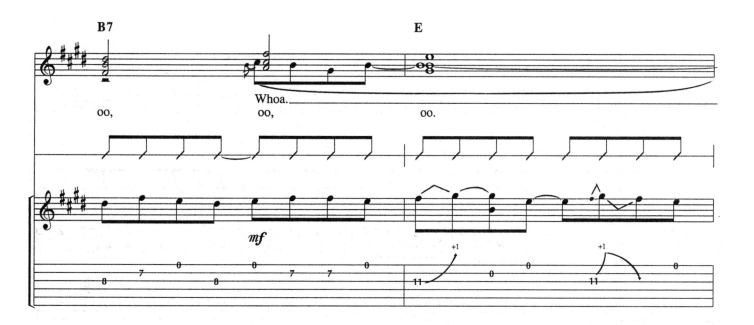

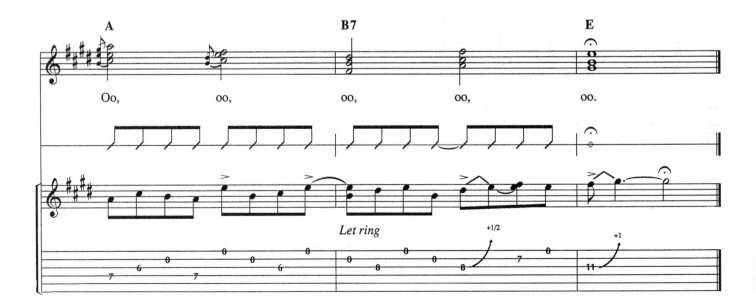

Take It Easy

Words and Music by
JACKSON BROWNE and GLENN FREY

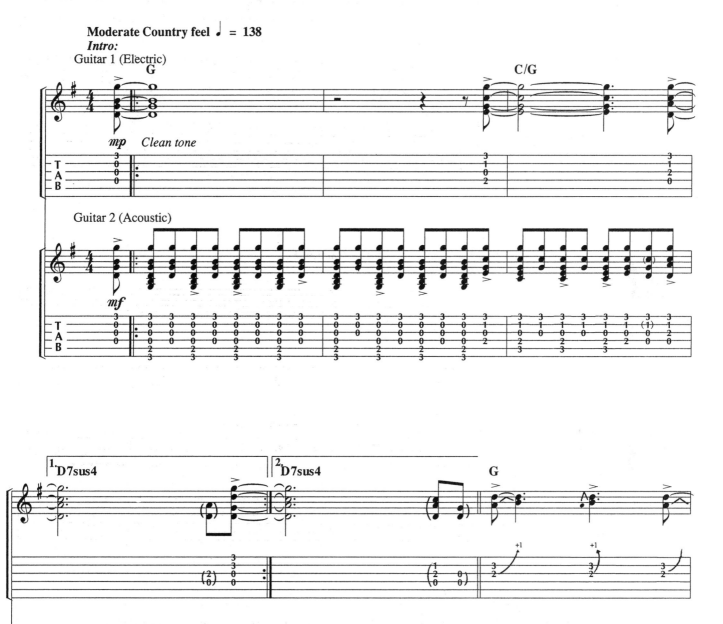

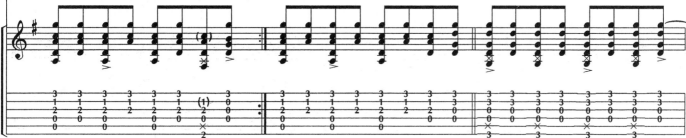

Guitar 3 plays upper voice.
Guitar 4 plays lower voice.

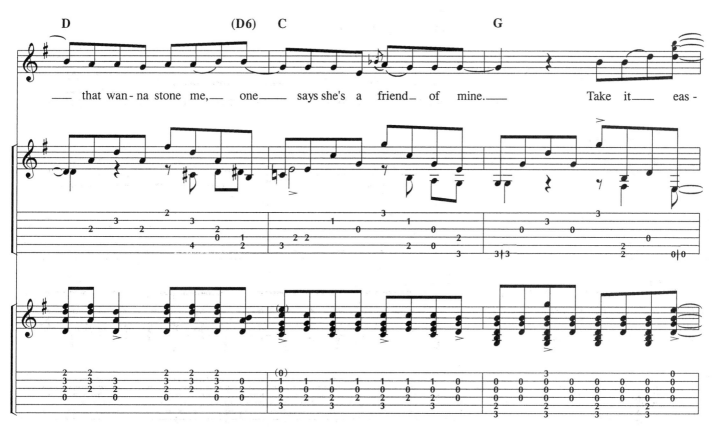

that wan-na stone me,___ one___ says she's a friend___ of mine.___ Take it___ eas-

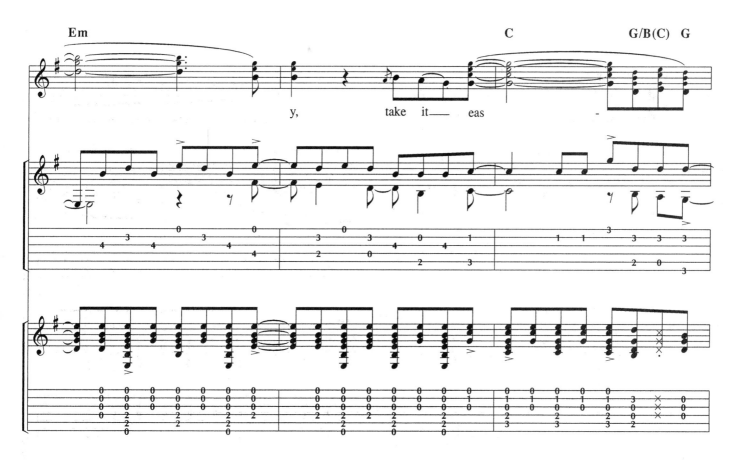

y, take it___ eas -

y, don't let the sound of your own wheels drive you cra-
Oo,_____

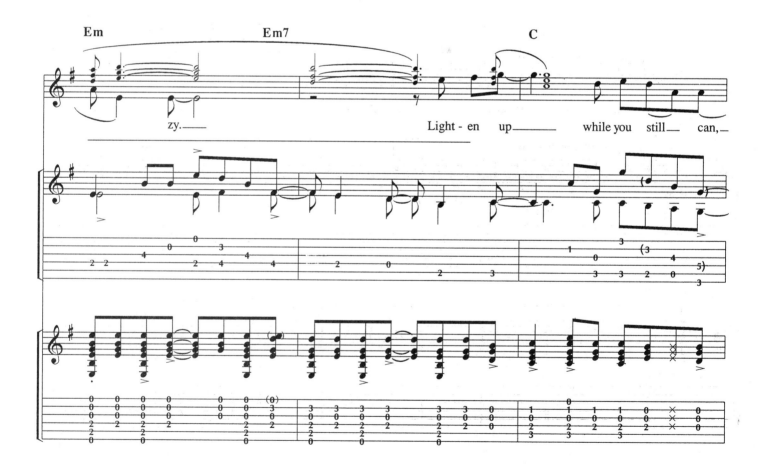

zy.____   Light-en up____ while you still__ can,__

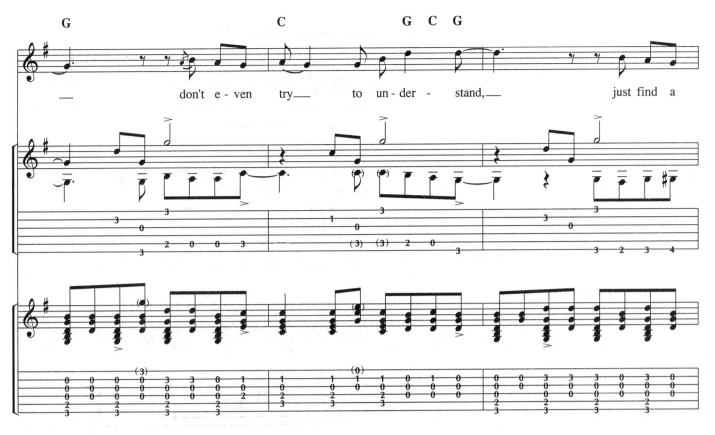

don't e - ven try___ to un - der - stand,___ just find a

place to make___ your___ stand___ an' take it eas -

Verse 2:

Guitar 2 simile voicings to Verse 1.

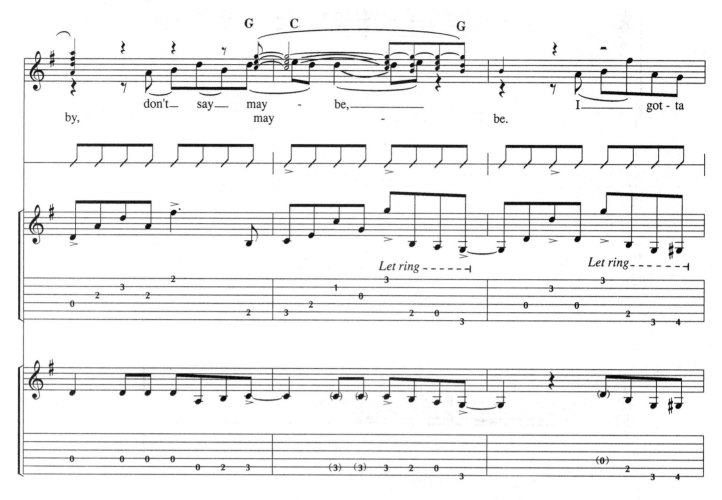

We may lose_____ and we may_____ win, though we will

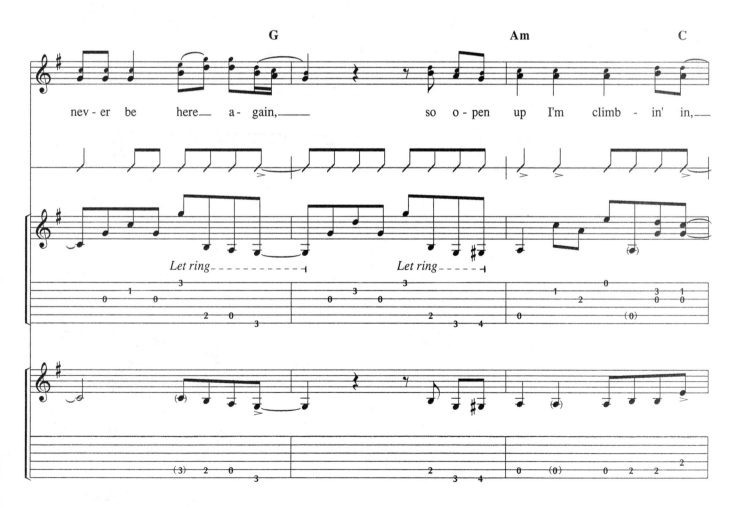

nev - er be here____ a - gain,_____ so o - pen up I'm climb - in' in,_____

114

so take it eas - y.

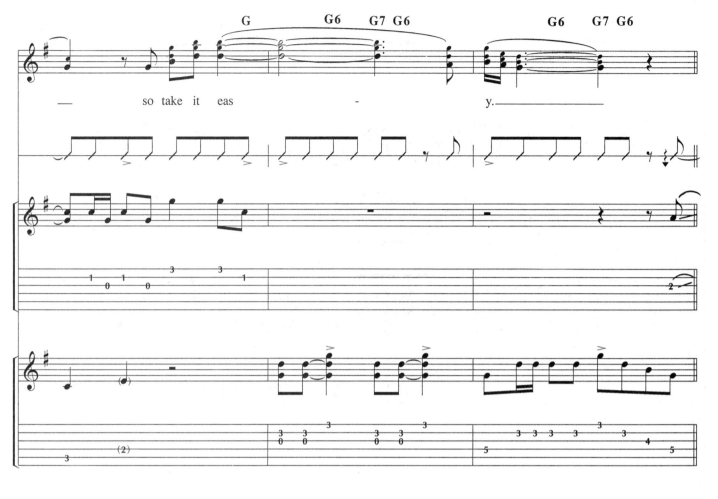

Guitar Solo

Guitar 2

Guitar 1   (Enter Banjo)

Let ring

Guitar 3 *(Guitar 4 tacet)*

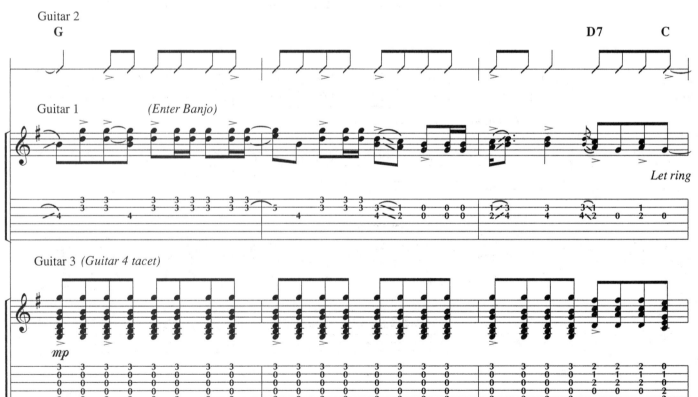

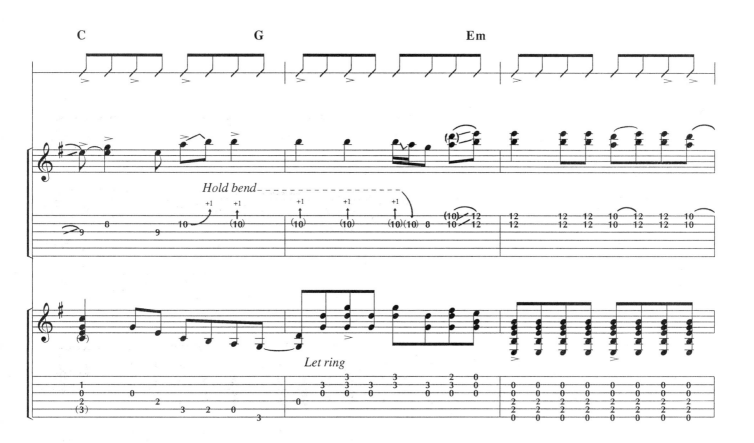

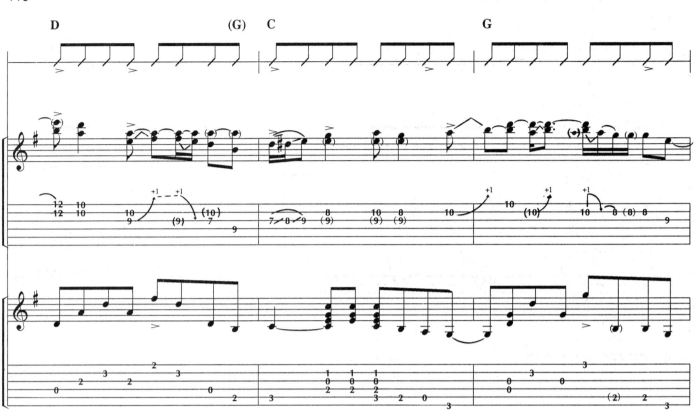

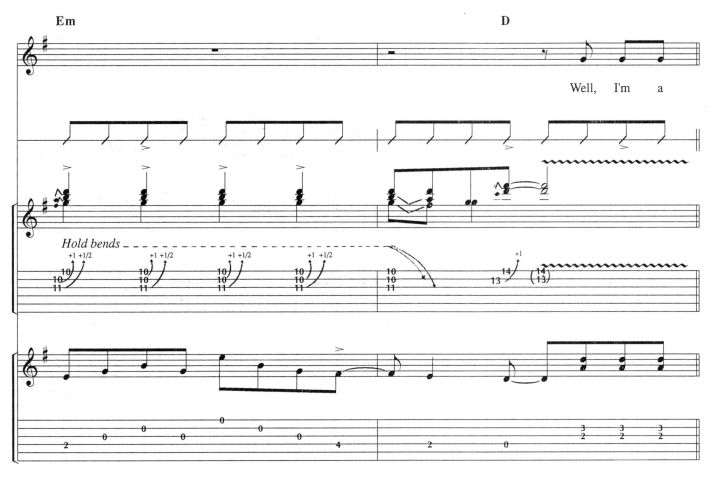

Well, I'm a

Verse 3:

run-nin' down the road try'n' to loos-en my load,____ got a world____

Oo,____

Guitar 2

Guitar 3

Guitar 4

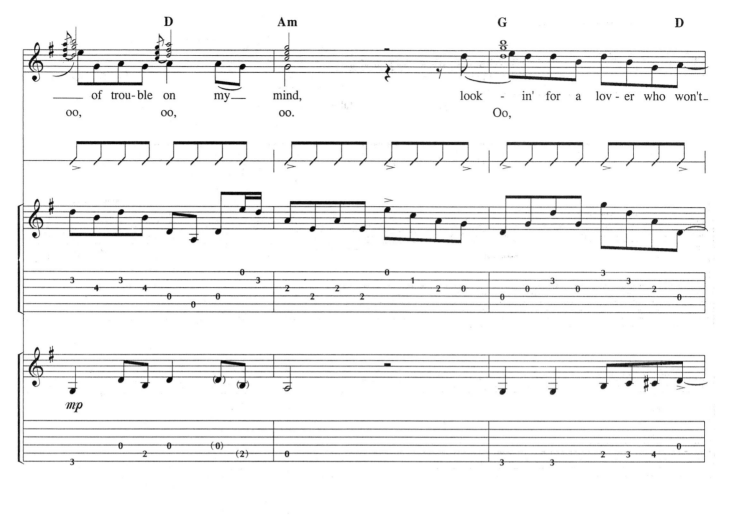

y, take it___ eas -

y, don't let the sound of your___ own___ wheels_____ make you

Oo,_____ oo,_____

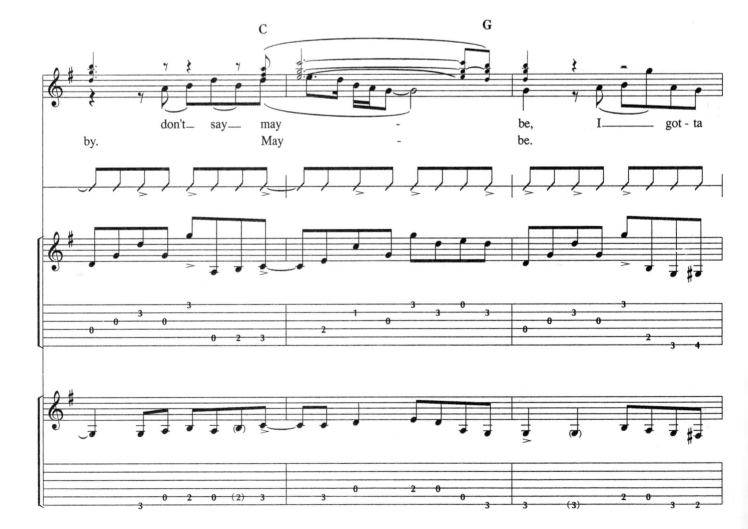

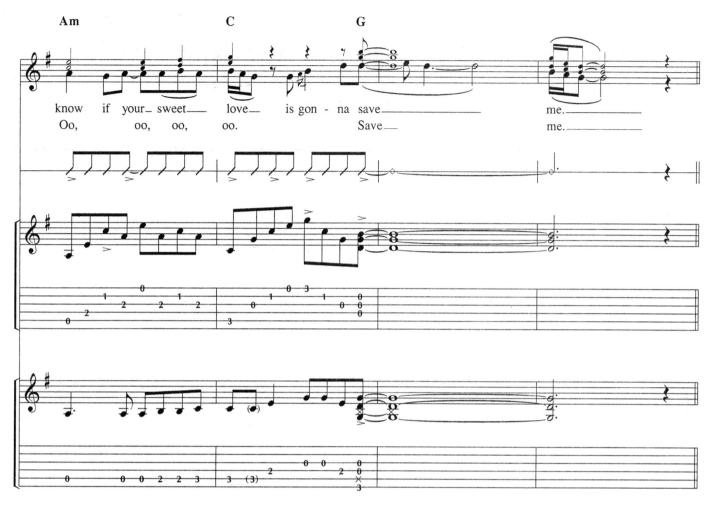

know if your sweet love is gon-na save me.
Oo, oo, oo, oo. Save me. Oo

Outro:

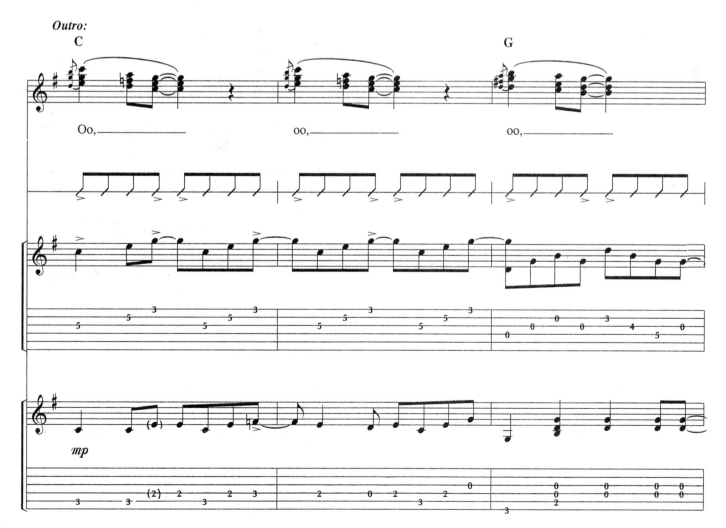

Oo, oo, oo,

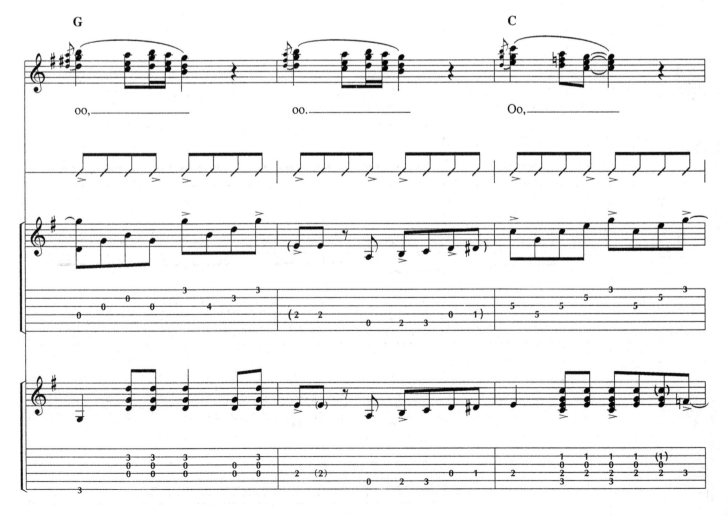

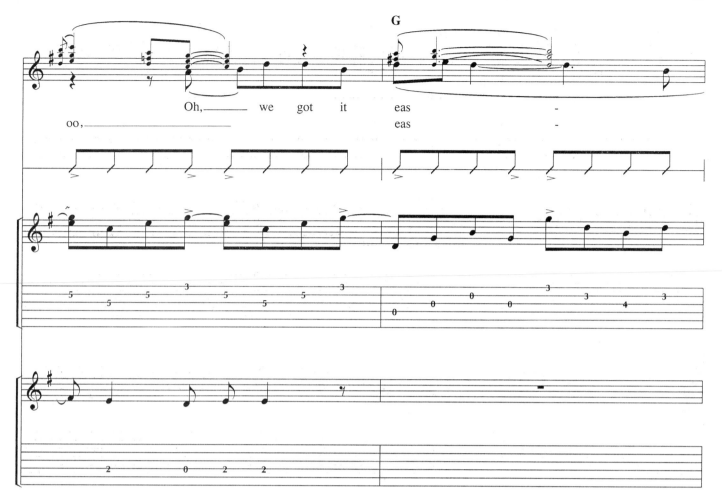

Oh,_____ we got it eas

oo,_____ eas -

y._____

y.

We ought to take it

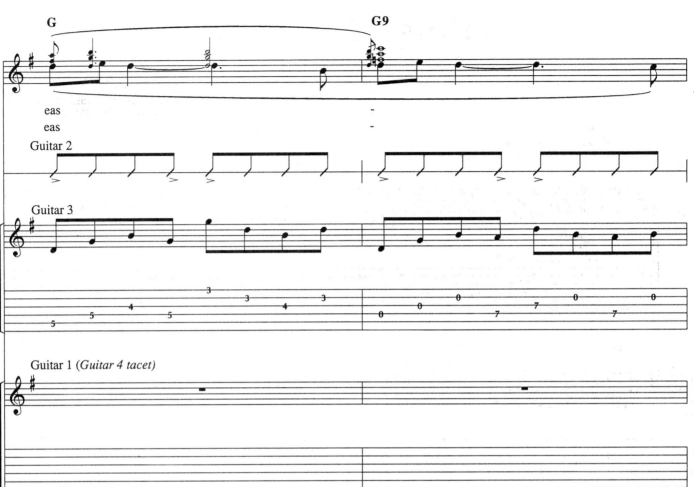

HOTEL CALIFORNIA

Words and Music by
**DON HENLEY, GLENN FREY
and DON FELDER**

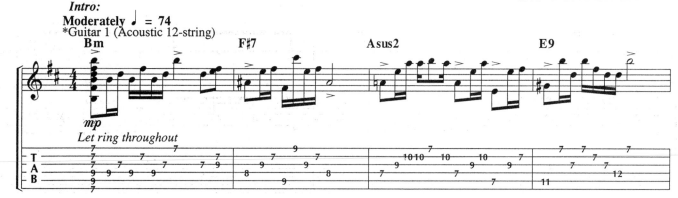

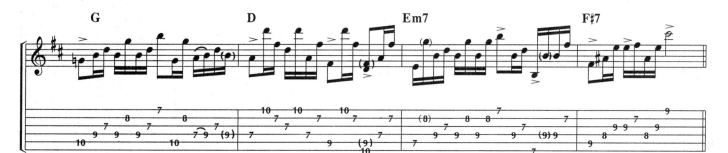

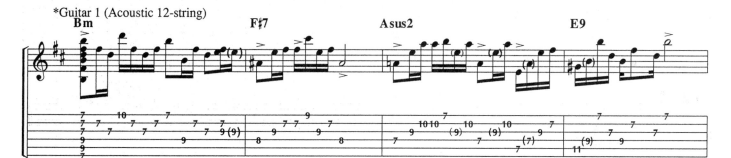

* *With capo at VII fret. Number 7 in tab represents capoed open string.*

Verse 1:

Guitar 5 plays upper voicing.
Guitar 6 plays lower voicing.

Chorus:

"Wel-come to the Ho - tel Cal - i - for - nia, such a

love - ly place_ (such a love - ly place)_ such a love - ly face._

Continued in slashes

* *Guitars 5 and 6*
** *Guitar 4*

Guitar 5 plays upper voice.
Guitar 6 plays lower voice.

**Guitar 4

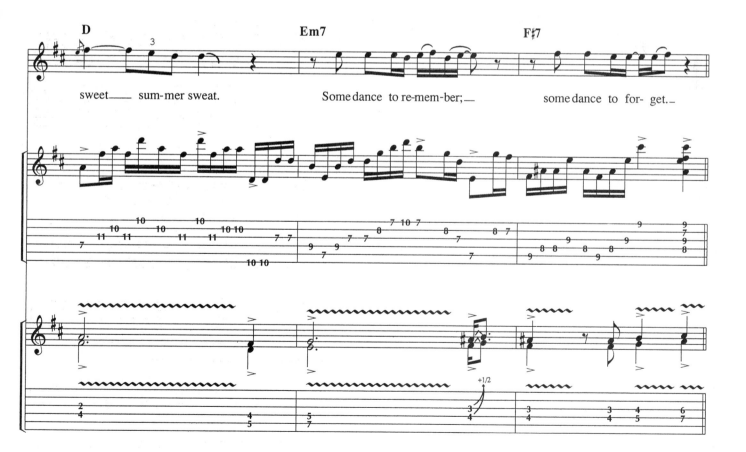

132

*Guitar 7 plays upper voice
Guitar 8 plays lower voice.

Chorus:

"Wel-come to the Ho-tel Cal-i-for-nia, such a

love-ly place (such a love-ly place) such a love-ly face. They're

*Guitars 5 and 6
**Guitar 4

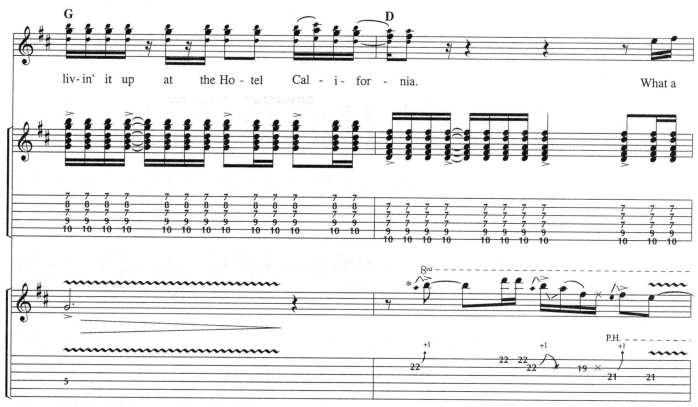

liv-in' it up   at   the Ho - tel   Cal - i - for - nia.   What a

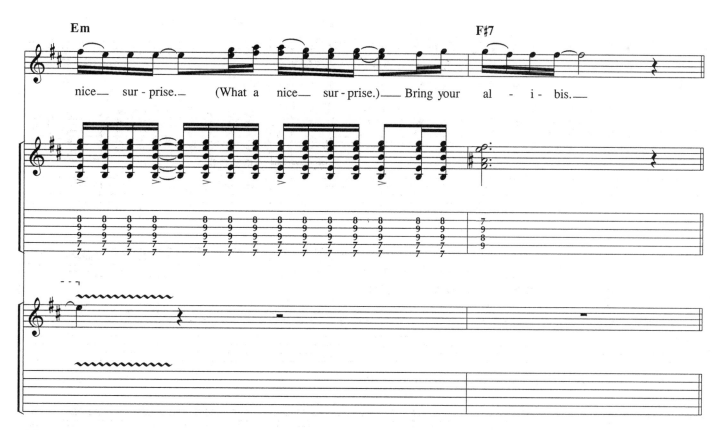

nice__ sur - prise.__ (What a   nice__ sur - prise.)__ Bring your   al - i - bis.__

*Guitar 4

Verse 5:

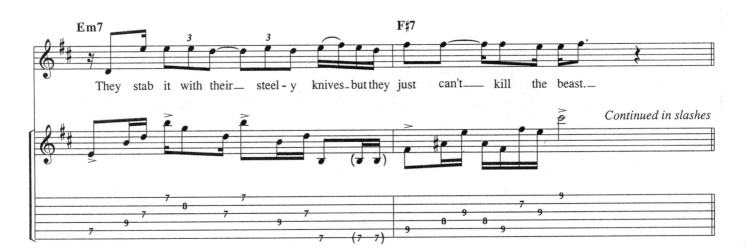

Verse 6:

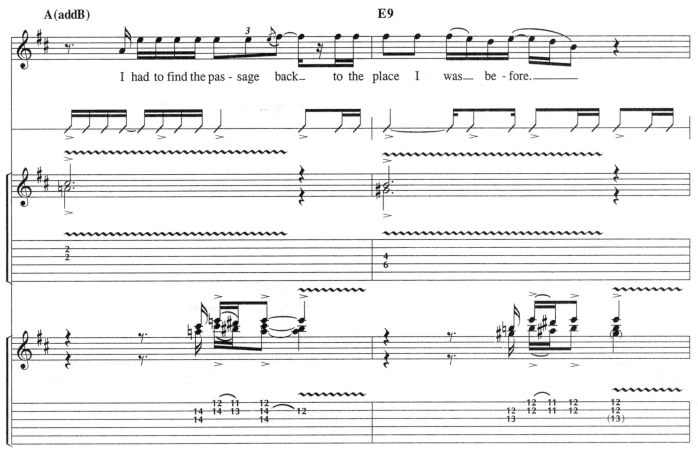

*Guitar 5 plays upper note, Guitar 6 plays lower note.
** Guitar 7 plays upper note, Guitar 8 plays lower note.

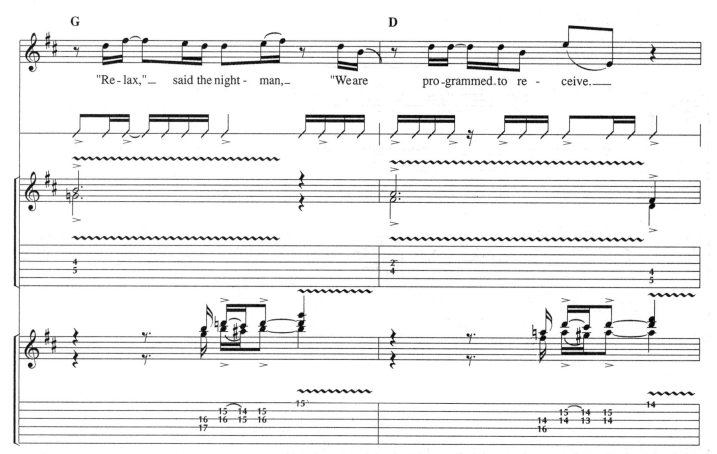

"Re - lax," said the night - man, "We are pro-grammed to re - ceive.

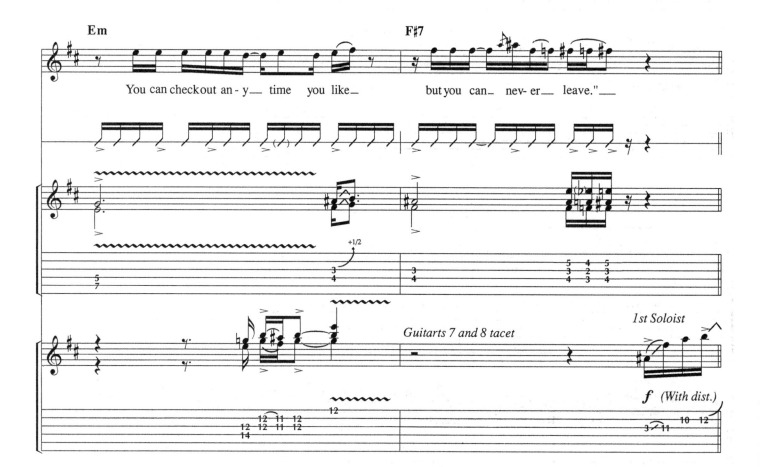

You can check out an - y time you like but you can nev- er leave."

Guitars 7 and 8 tacet

1st Soloist

f (With dist.)

Guitar Solo With Rhythm Figures 1, 2, and 3 (3 times)

Guitars 5 and 6

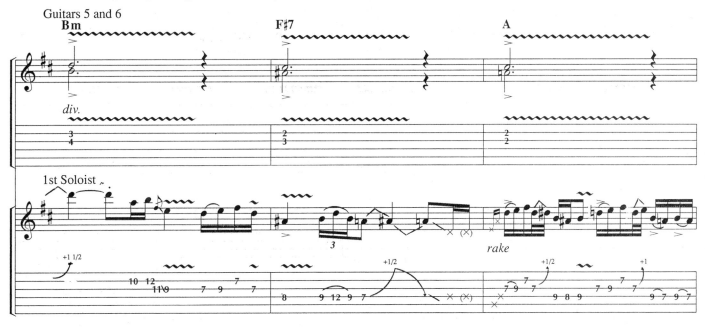

1st Soloist

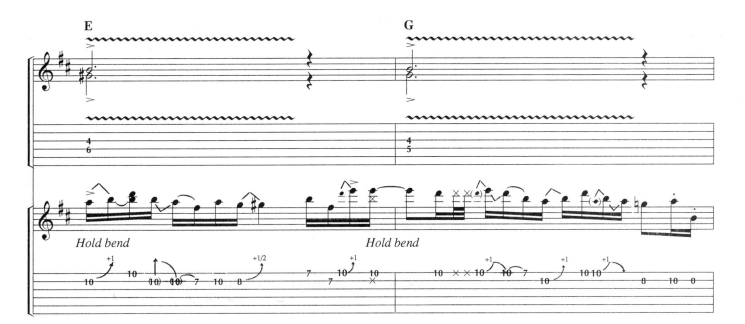

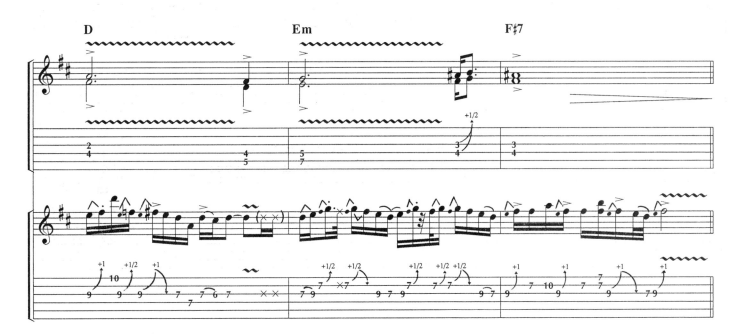

140

*Open string noise.
** Echo repeat
*** 1st soloist plays lower note.

142

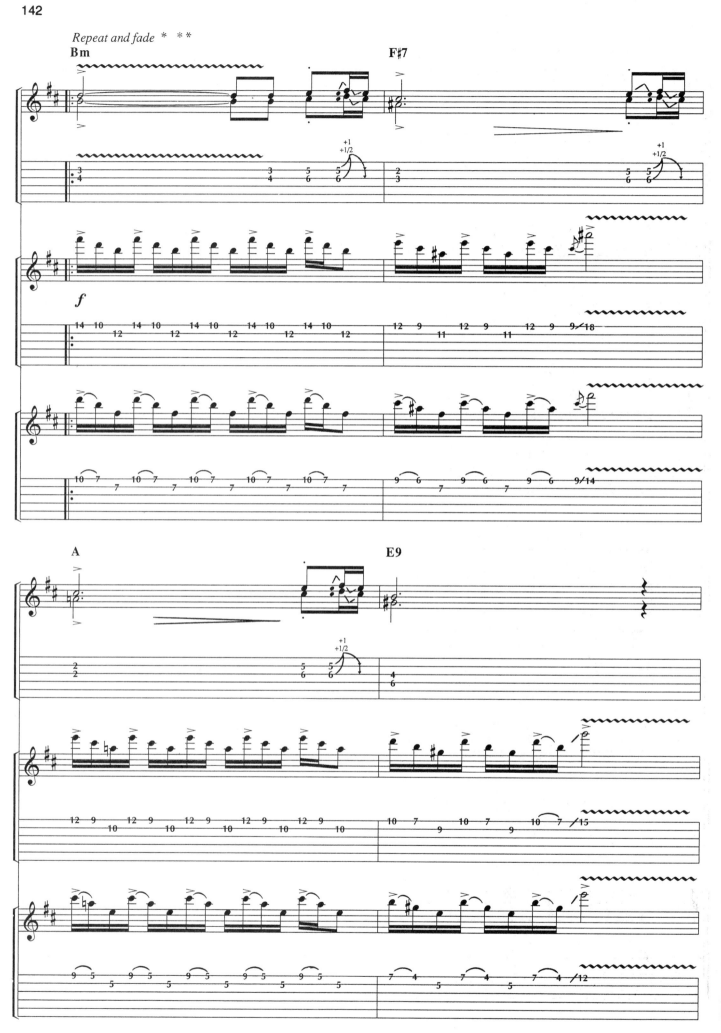

* Guitars 3 and 4 tacet.
** With Rhythm Figure 3 - ad lib.

LYIN' EYES

Words and Music by
DON HENLEY and GLENN FREY

* Guitar 2 doubled with 6 - string guitar capoed at 5th fret.

Verse 1:

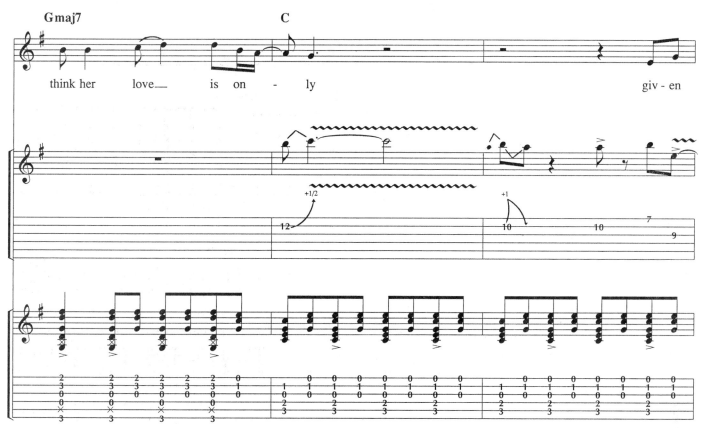

think her love— is on - ly giv - en

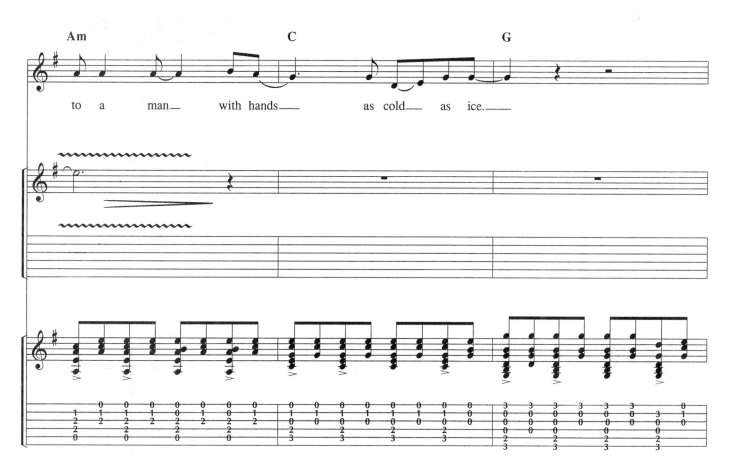

to a man— with hands— as cold— as ice.—

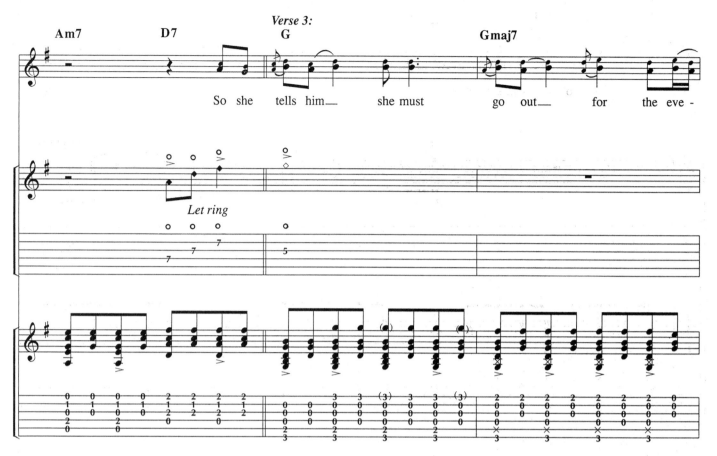

So she tells him___ she must go out___ for the eve -

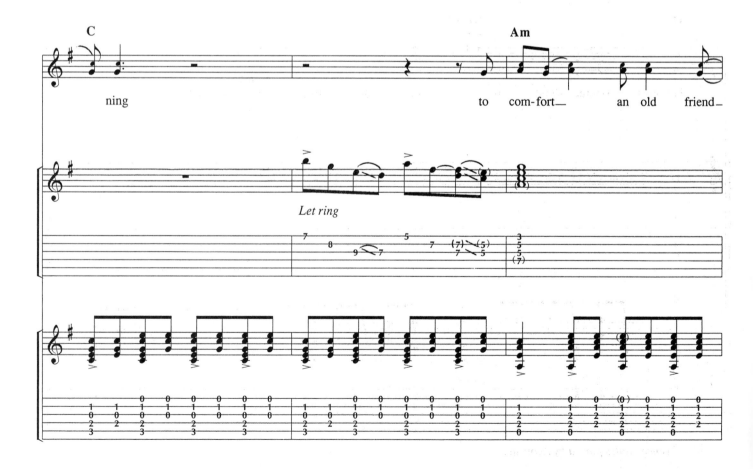

ning to com-fort___ an old friend___

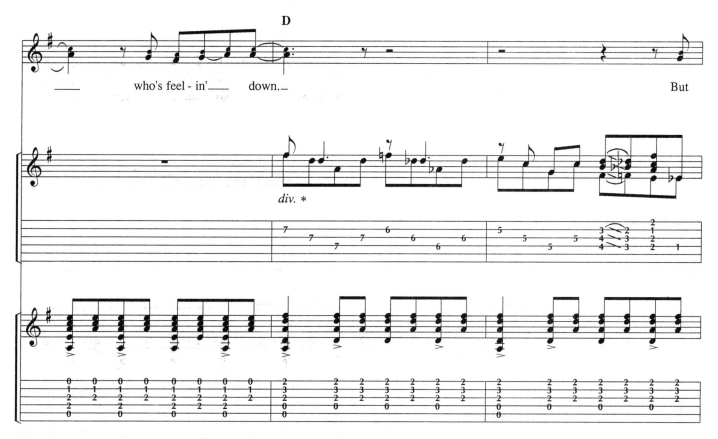

who's feel-in' down.___ But

*div. ***

he knows where__ she's go - in' as she's leav - in';

* Lower stemmed notes played by Acoustic.

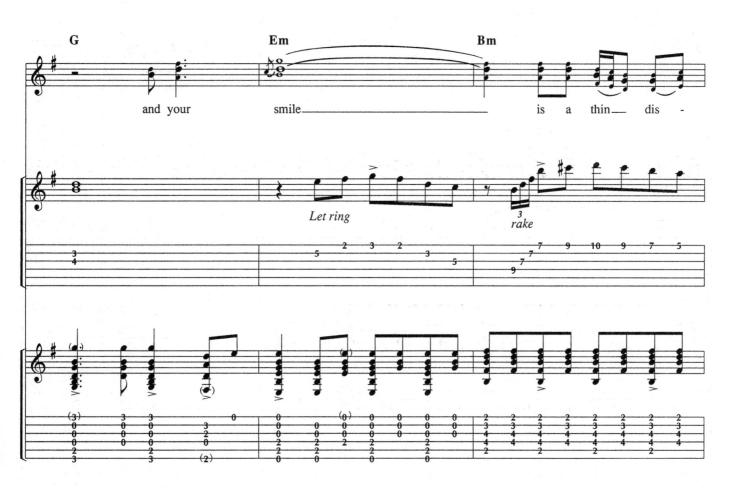

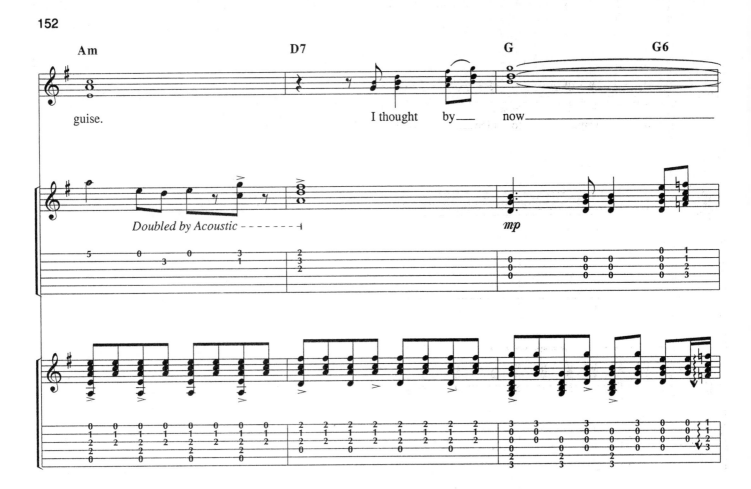

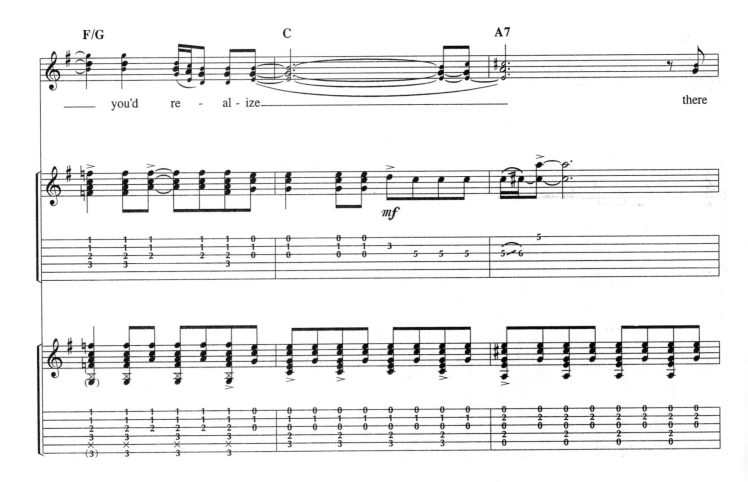

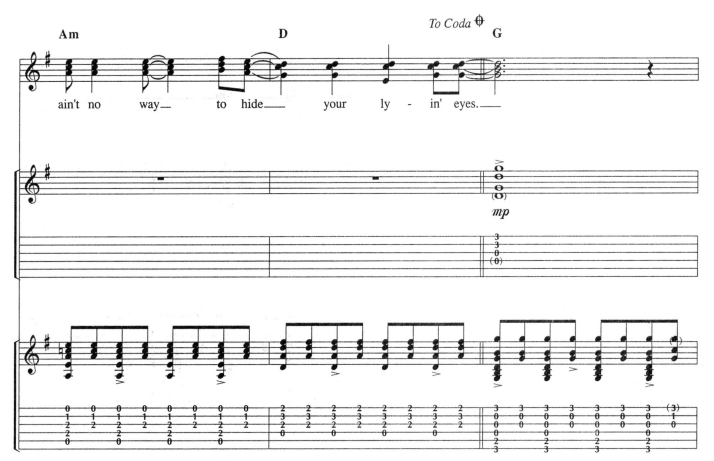

ain't no way___ to hide___ your ly - in' eyes.___

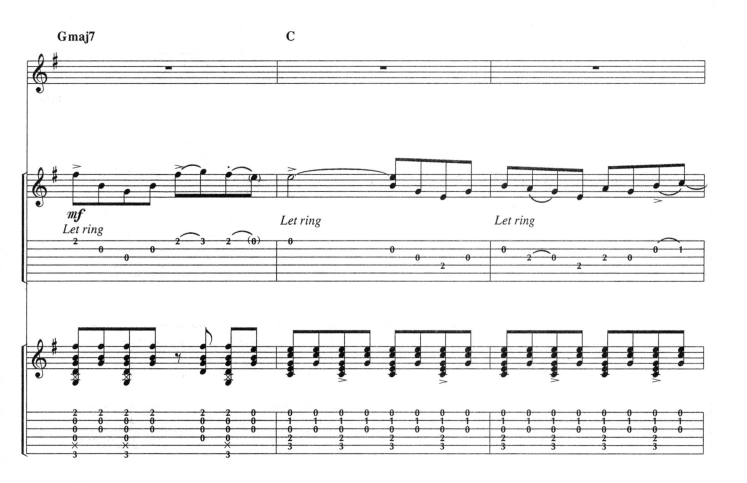

154

* *Up stemmed notes*

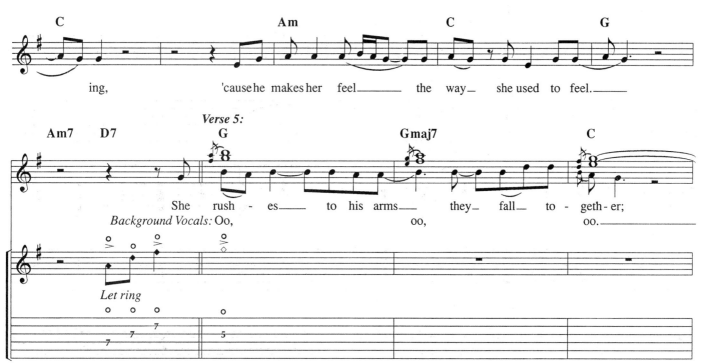

C   Am   C   G

ing,   'cause he makes her feel_____ the way_ she used to feel._____

Am7   D7   *Verse 5:*   G   Gmaj7   C

She rush - es_____ to his arms_____ they_ fall_ to - geth - er;

Background Vocals: Oo,   oo,   oo._____

Let ring

Am

she whis - pers_____ that it's on - ly_____ for a

Oo,_____

D7   G

while._   She swears that soon_ she'll be

oo._____   Oo,

Let ring

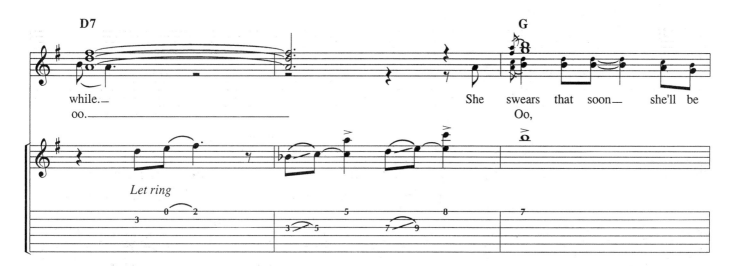

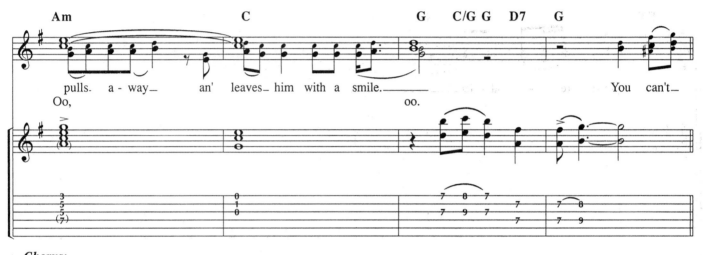

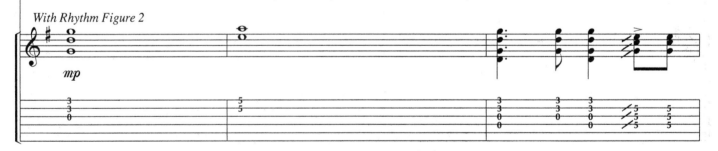

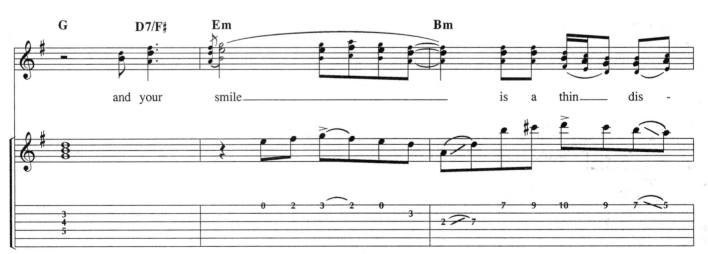

Verse 6:

She gets up___ an' pours___ her-self___ a strong___ one,

an' stares out at the stars___ up in the___ sky.___

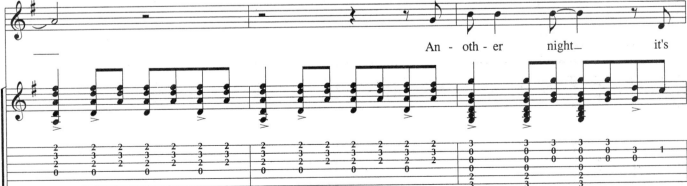

An - oth - er night___ it's

she knew in____ school.____ oo. ____ Did

Mandolin arranged for Guitar -

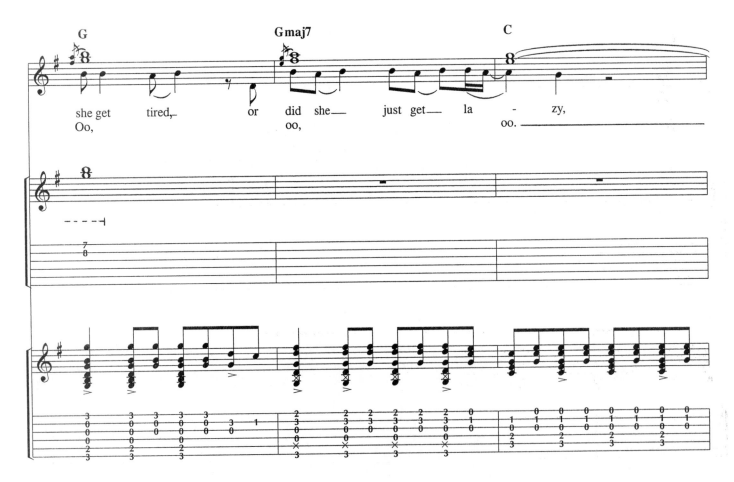

she get tired,____ or did she____ just get____ la - zy,

Oo, oo, oo. ____

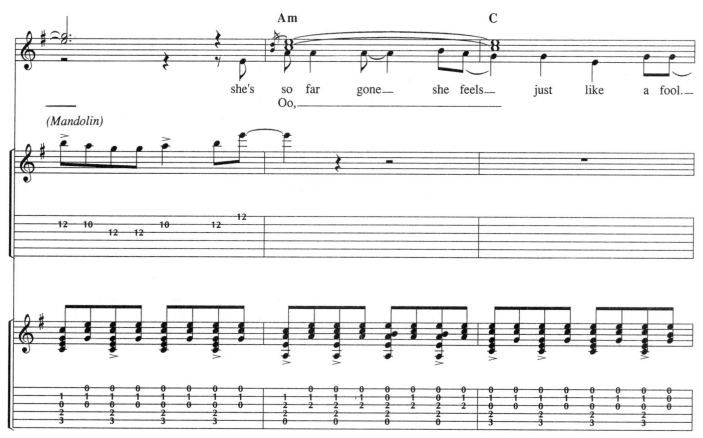

she's so far gone___ she feels___ just like a fool.___
Oo,___

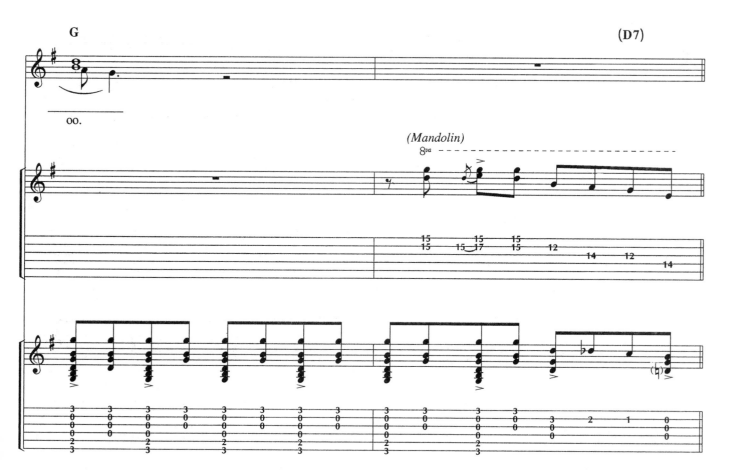

oo.

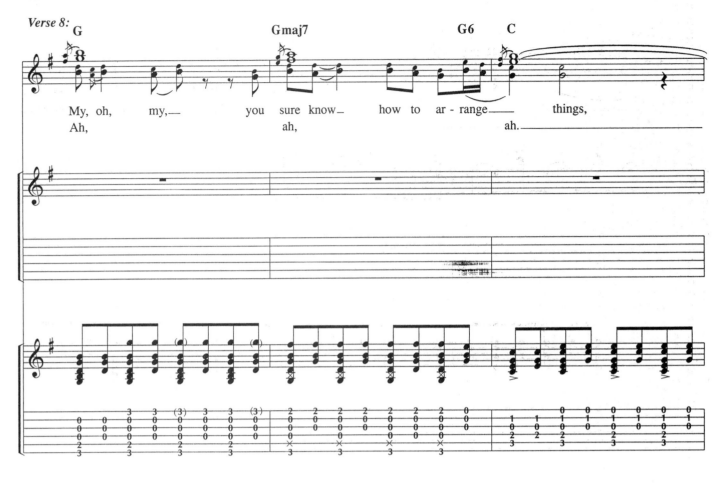

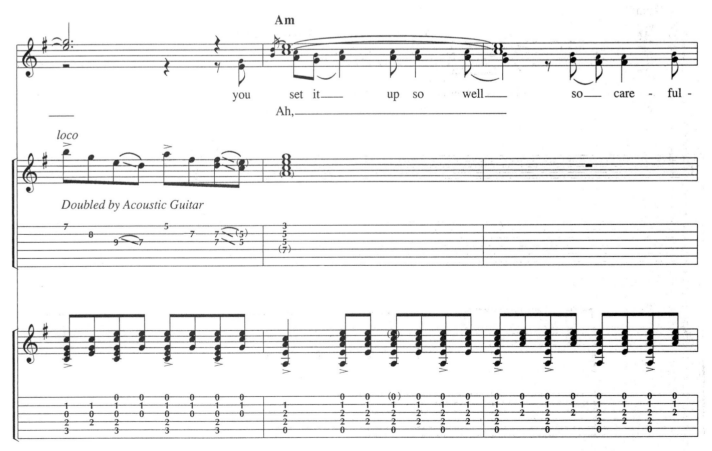

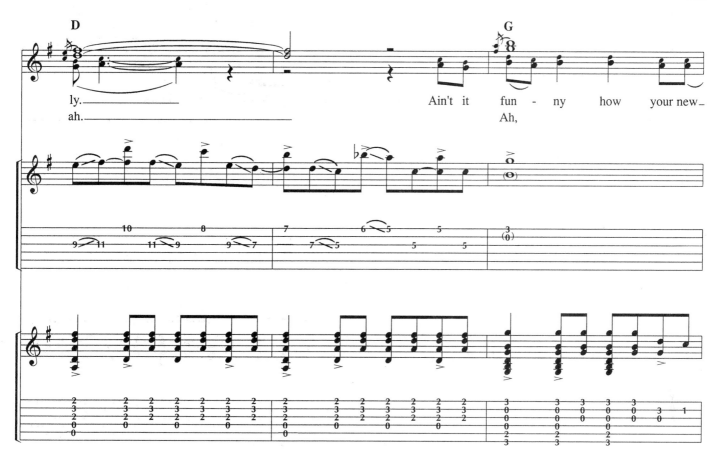

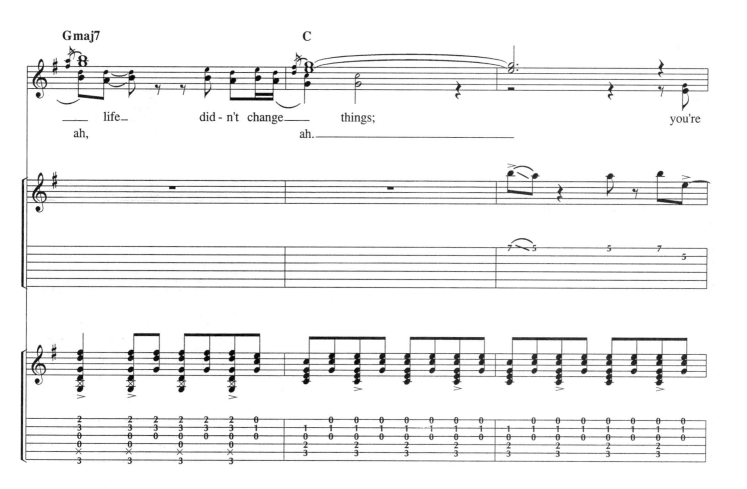

still the same old girl you used to be.
Ah, ah, ah.

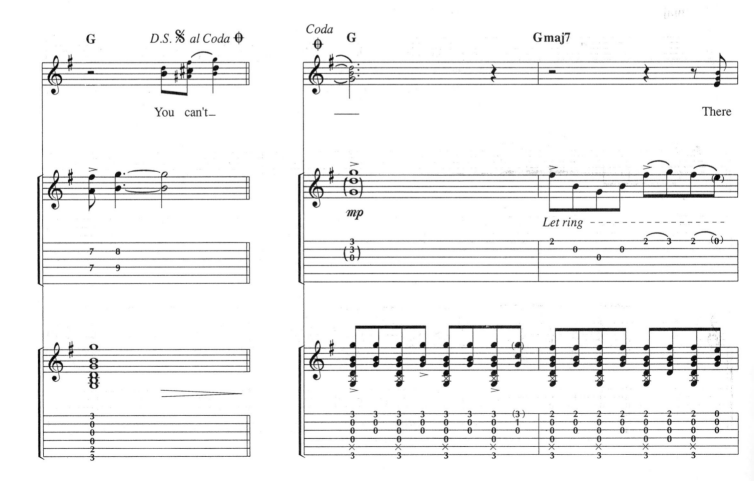

D.S. 𝄉 al Coda ⊕

You can't

Coda
⊕ G

Gmaj7

There

mp

Let ring - - - - - - - - - - - - - - - -

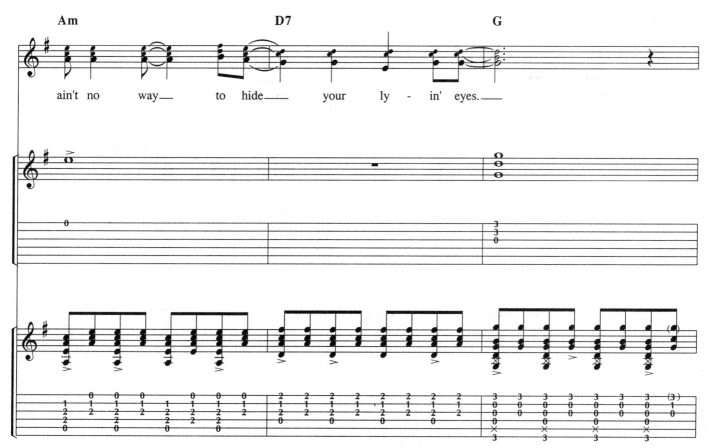

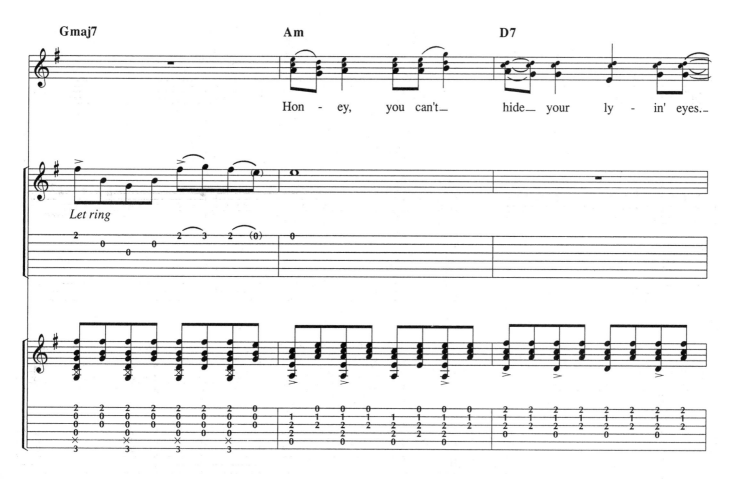

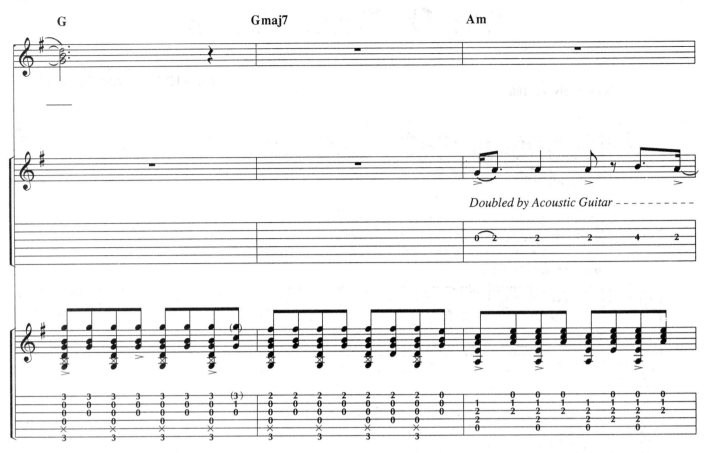

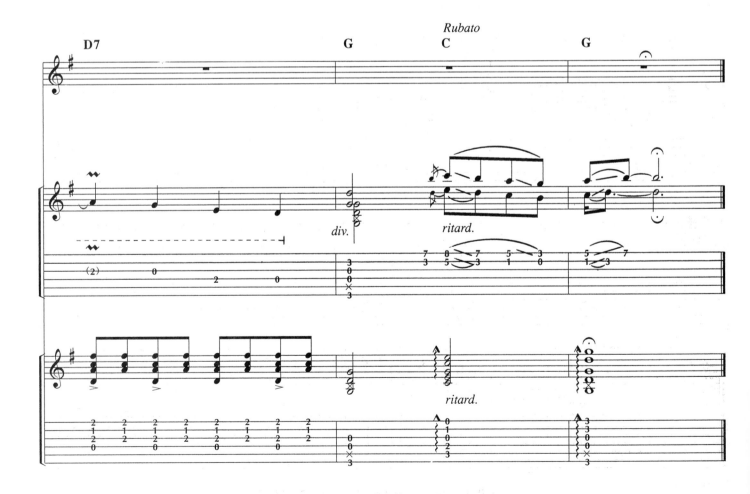

ONE OF THESE NIGHTS

Words and Music by
DON HENLEY and GLENN FREY

*Upstroke

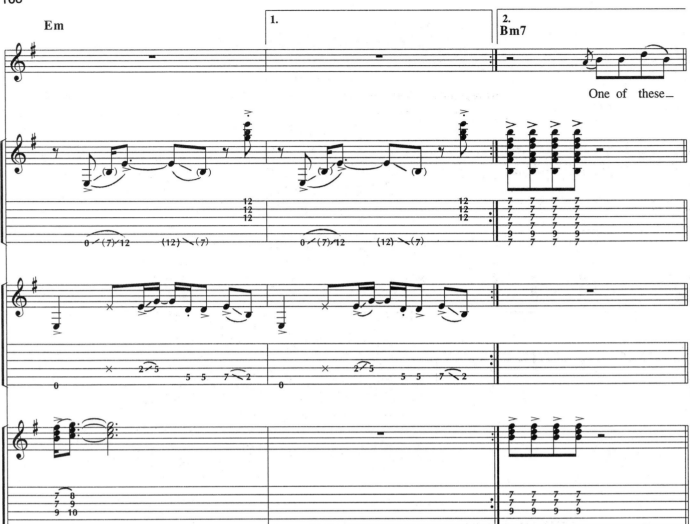

One of these_

Verse 1: *Rhythm Figure 1 (All Guitars)*

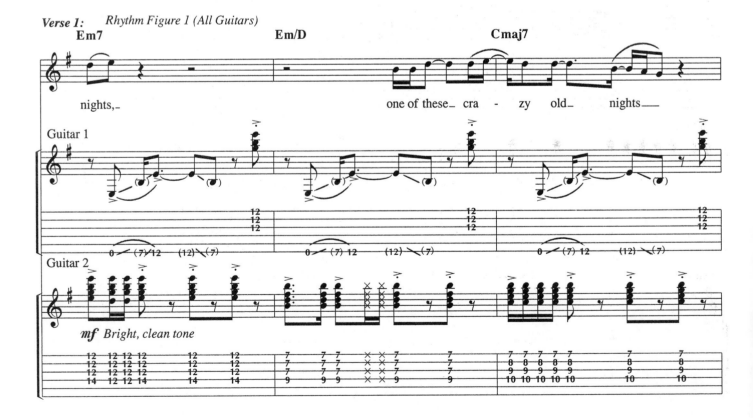

nights,_ one of these_ cra - zy old_ nights___

Guitar 1

Guitar 2

mf Bright, clean tone

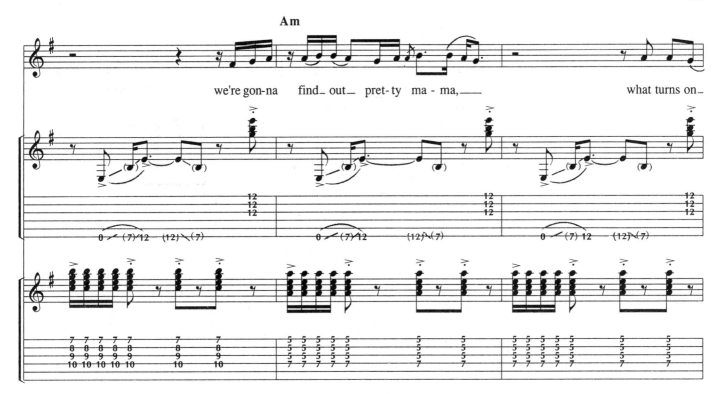

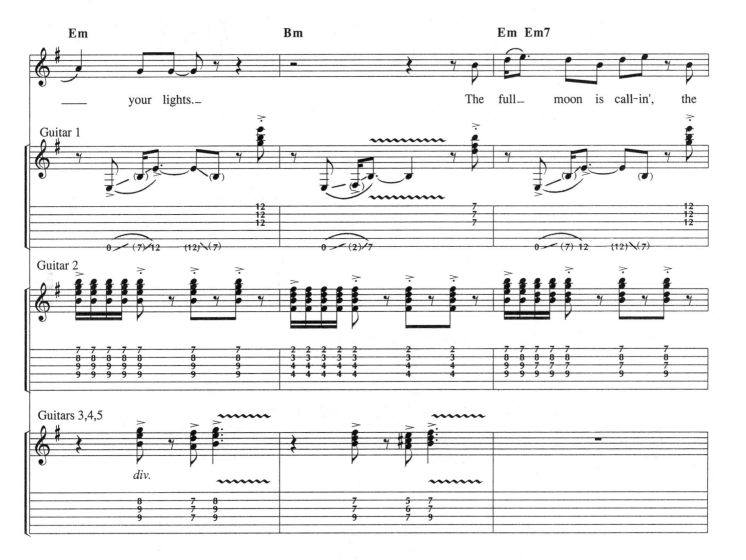

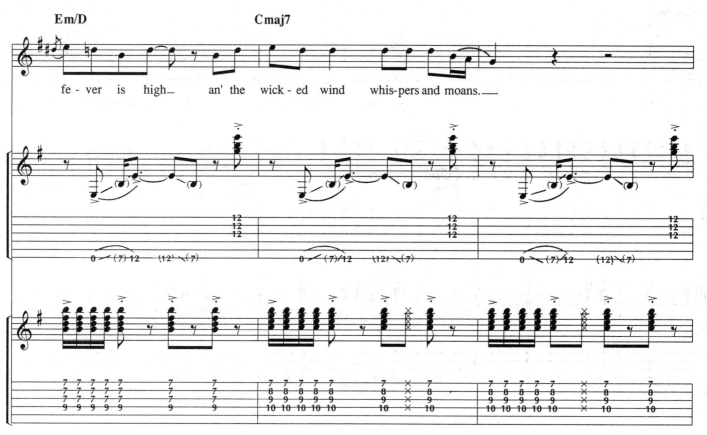

End Rhythm Figure 1

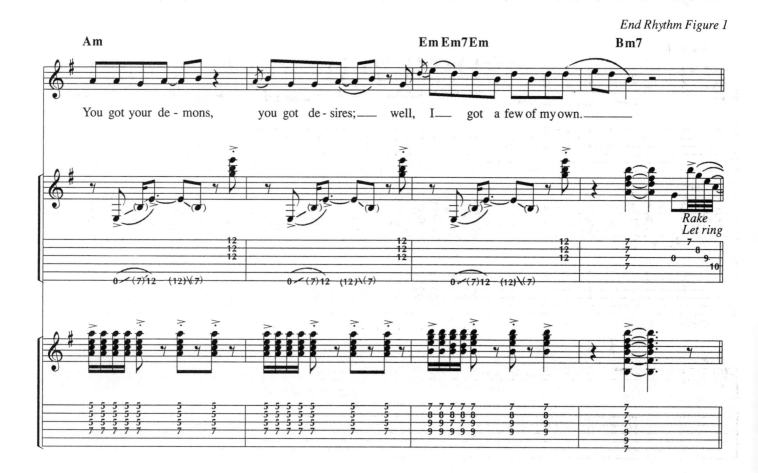

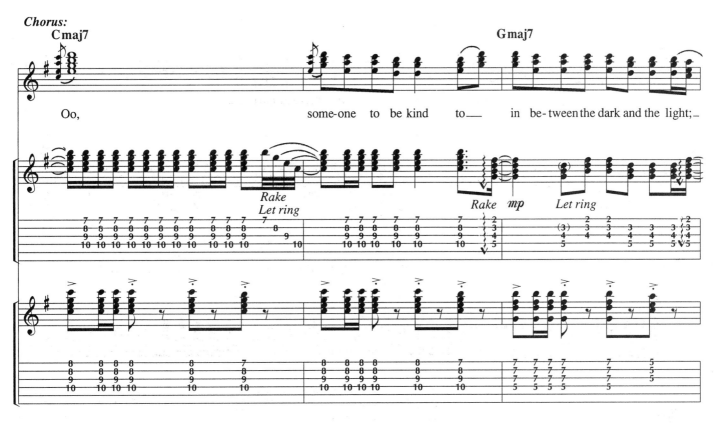

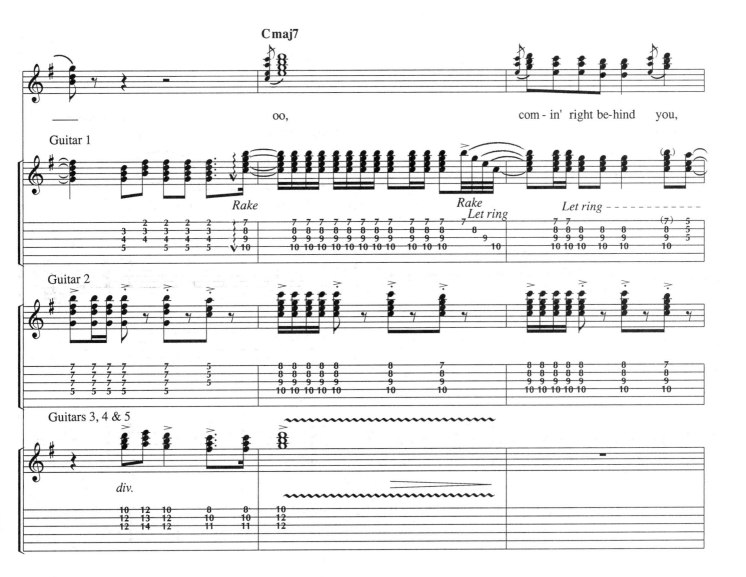

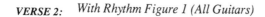

VERSE 2: *With Rhythm Figure 1 (All Guitars)*

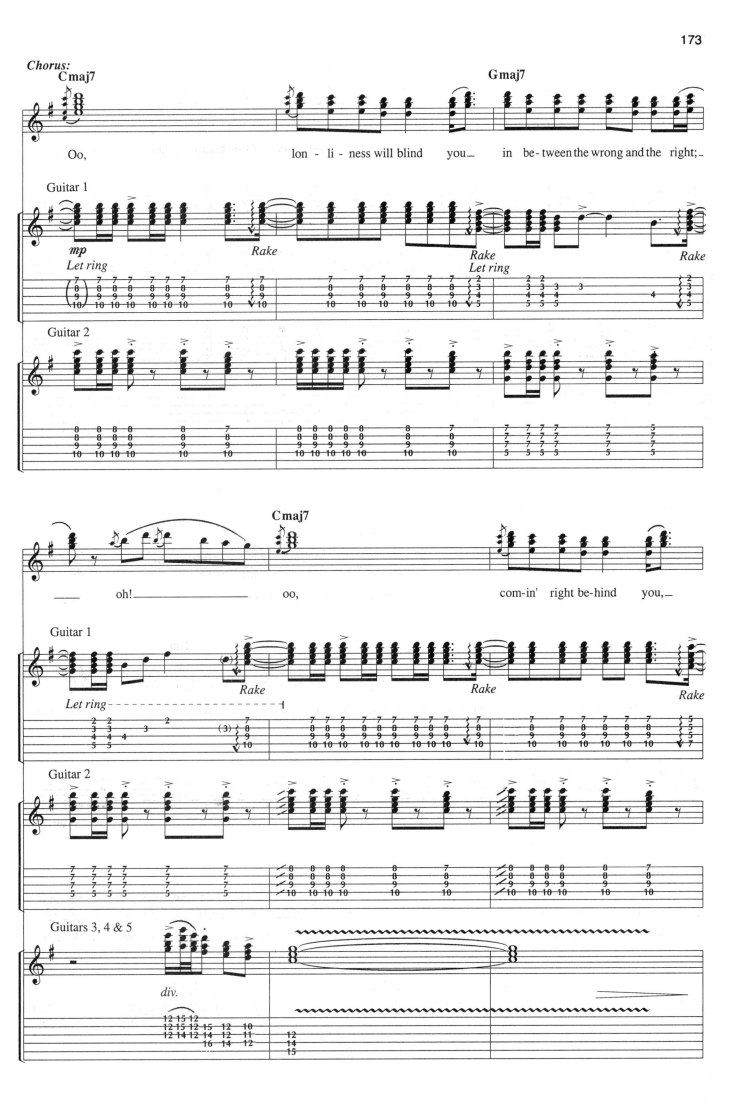

swear I'm gon - na find you___ one of these nights.___

(D)

Guitar 6

With distortion

Guitar Solo *With Rhythm Figure 1 (Guitars 1 - 5)*

* *Do not pick*

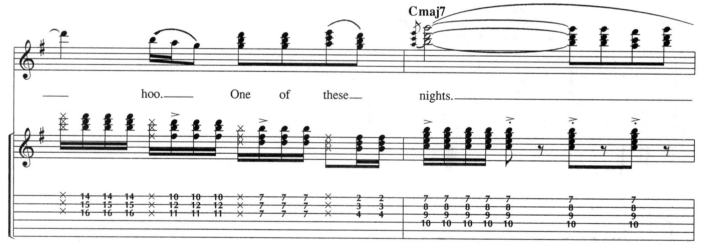

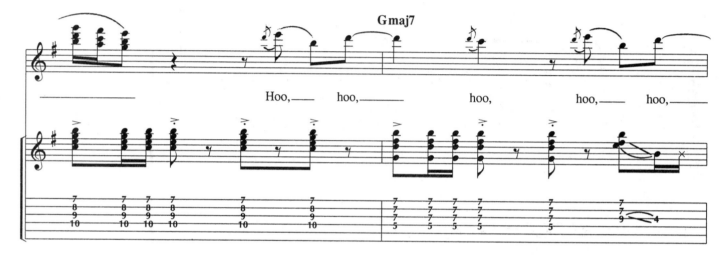

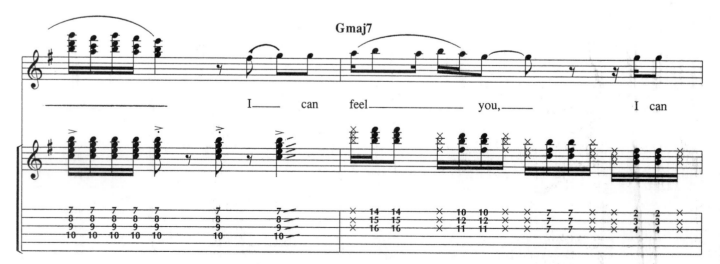

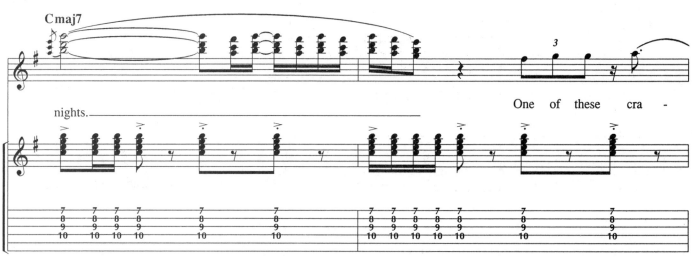

One of these cra -

zy, cra - zy, cra - zy nights._____ One of these_____

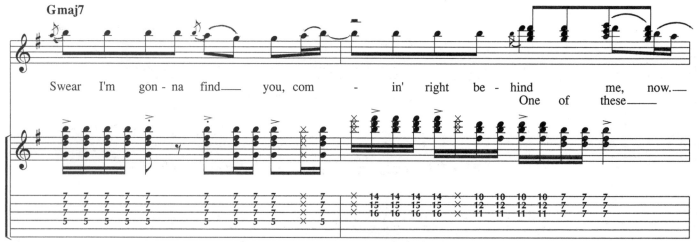

nights.

Swear I'm gon - na find____ you, com - in' right be - hind me, now.____ One of these_____

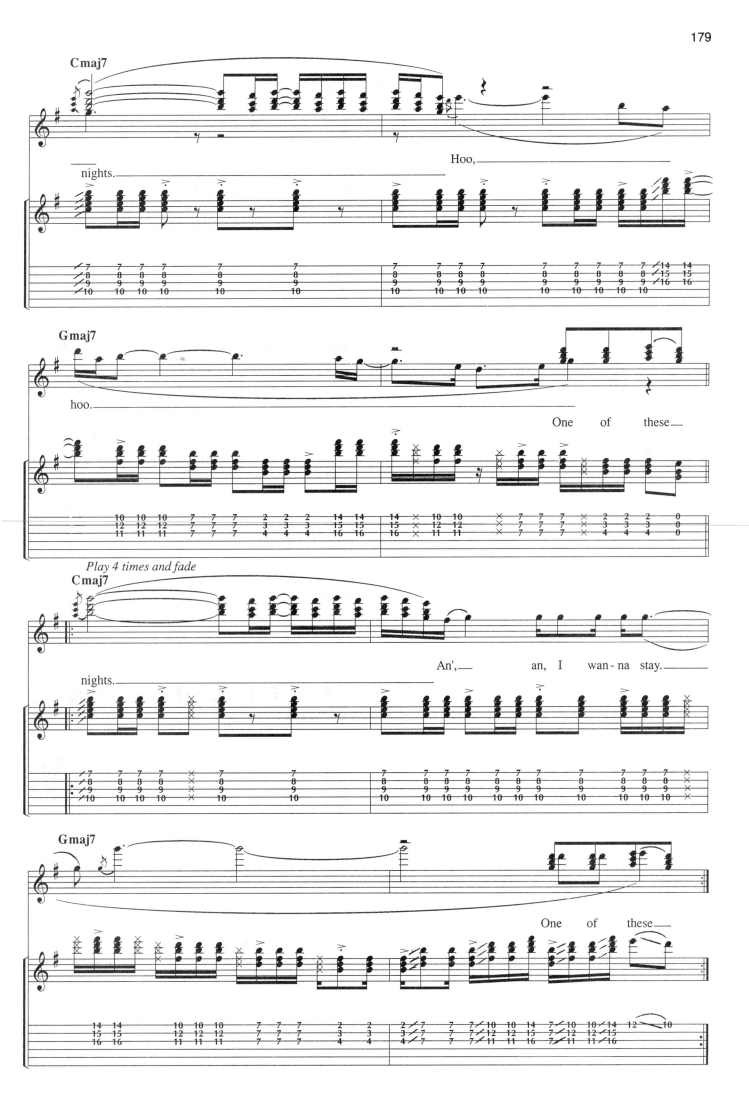

Take It To The Limit

Words and Music by
DON HENLEY, GLENN FREY
and RANDY MEISNER

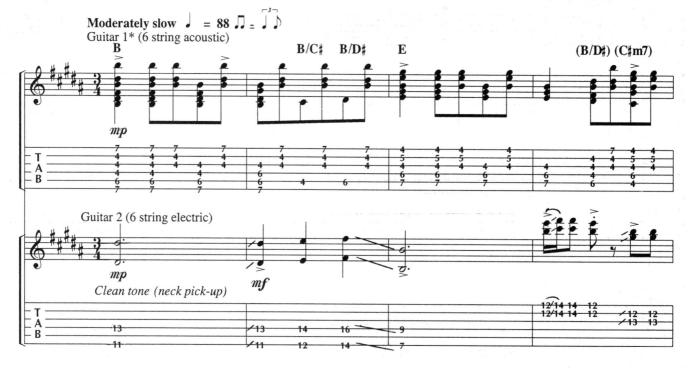

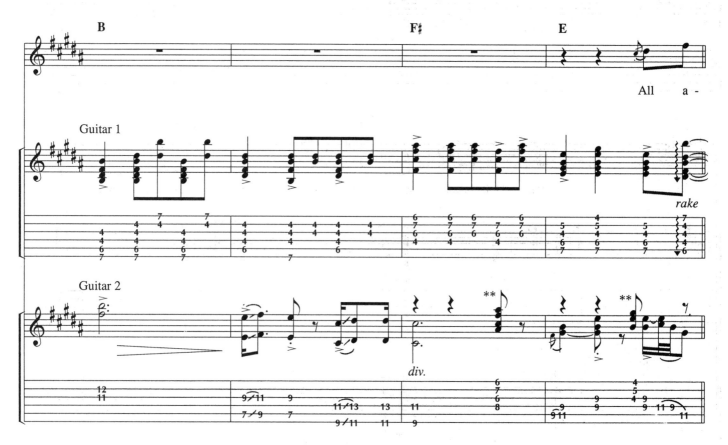

* With capo at 4th fret. Number 4 in TAB represents capoed open string.

** Guitar 3 (Electric) bridge pick-up

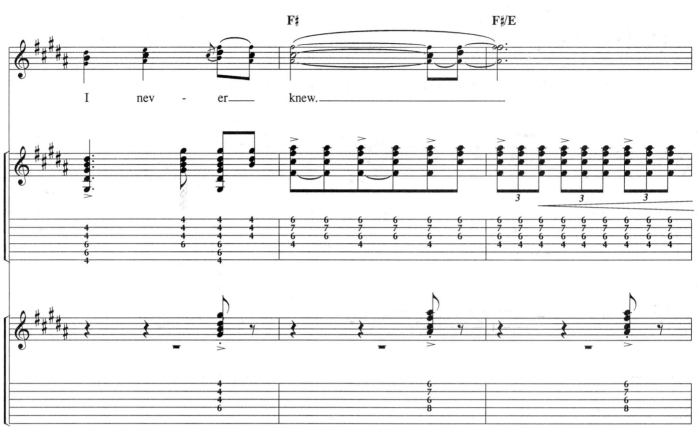

I nev - er___ knew.___

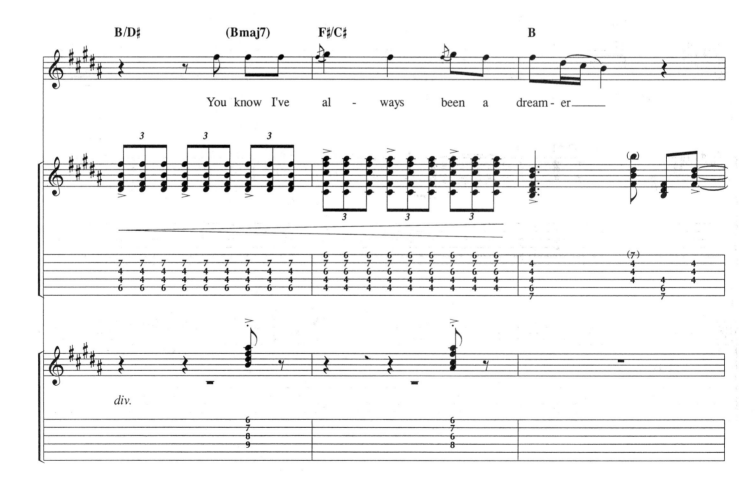

You know I've al - ways been a dream - er___

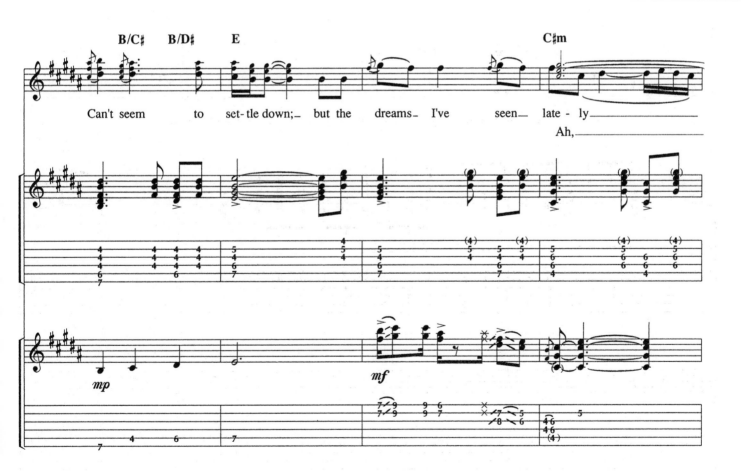

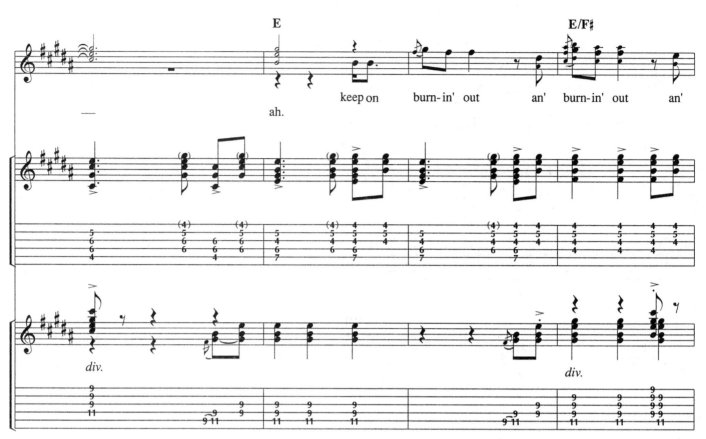

keep on burn-in' out an' burn-in' out an'
ah.

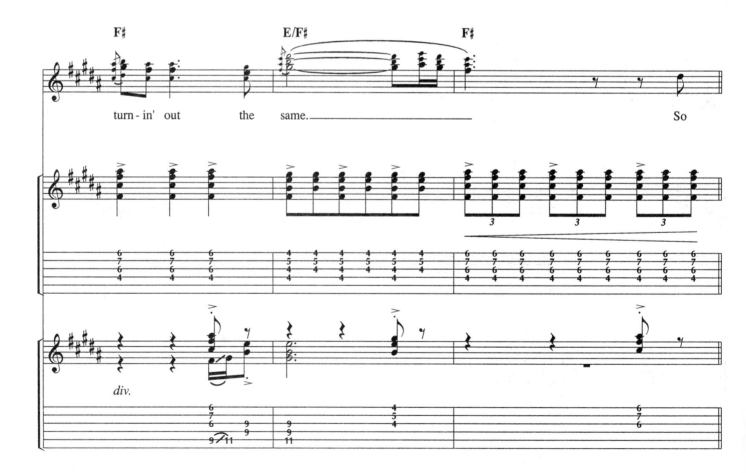

turn-in' out the same._____ So

Chorus:

put me— on a high-way— an' show— me a sign,— an'

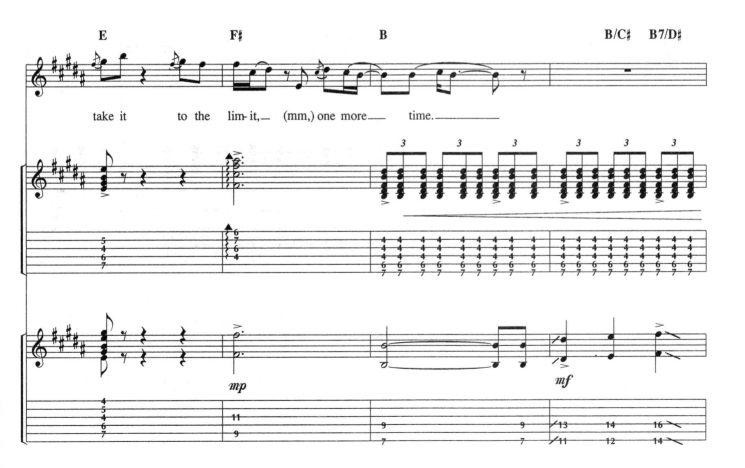

take it to the lim-it,— (mm,) one more— time.

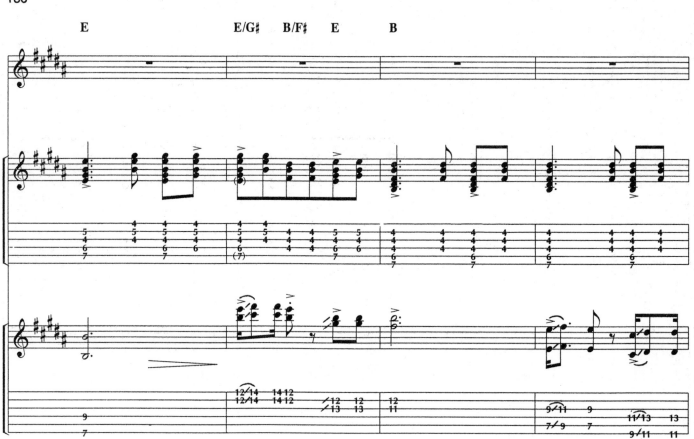

Verse 2:

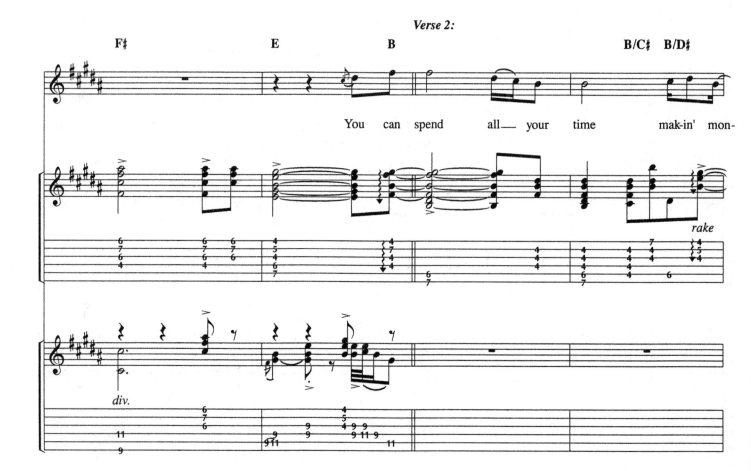

You can spend all— your time mak-in' mon-

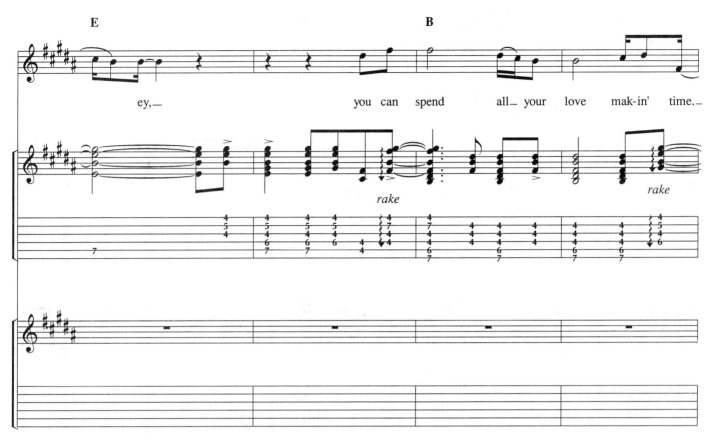

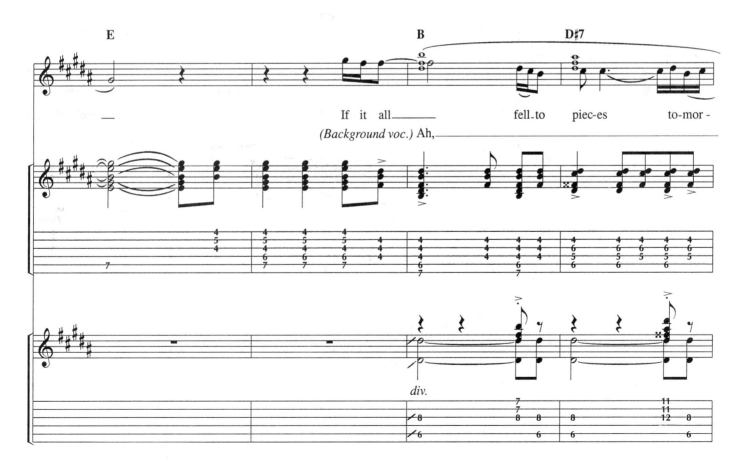

row would you still be___ mine?

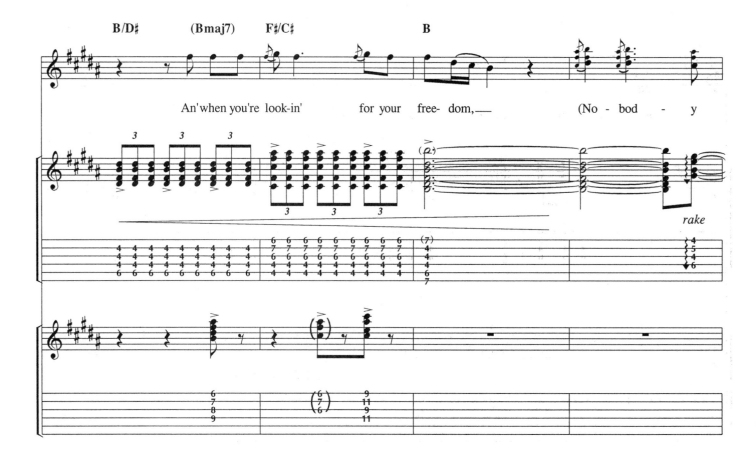

An'when you're look-in' for your free- dom,___ (No - bod - y

seems to care) and you can't find— the door,— (can't find it

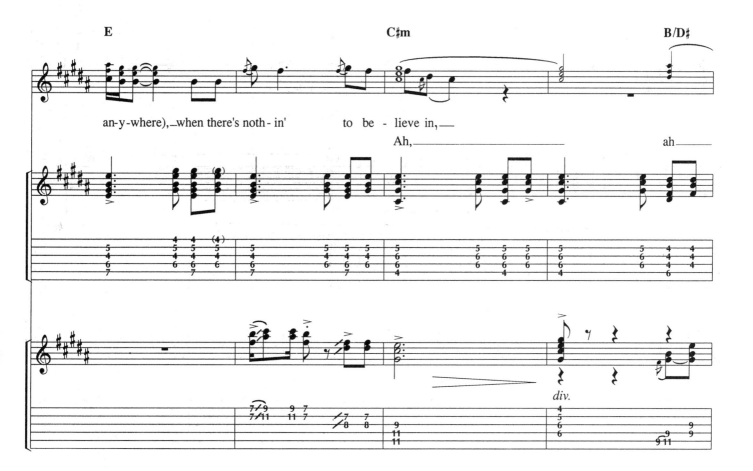

an-y-where),—when there's noth-in' to be - lieve in,—

Ah,———————— ah———

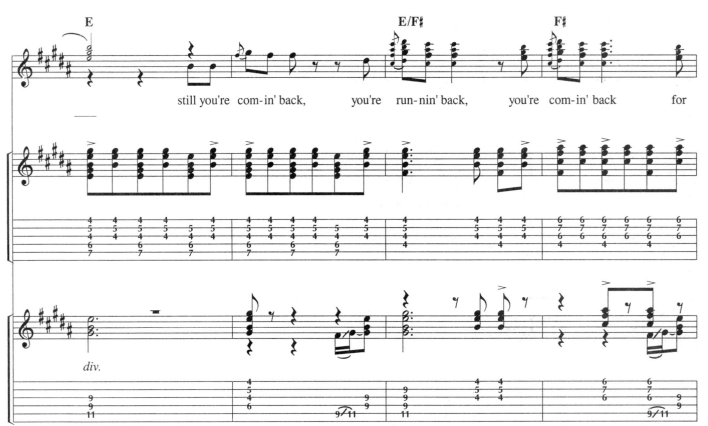

still you're com-in' back, you're run-nin' back, you're com-in' back for

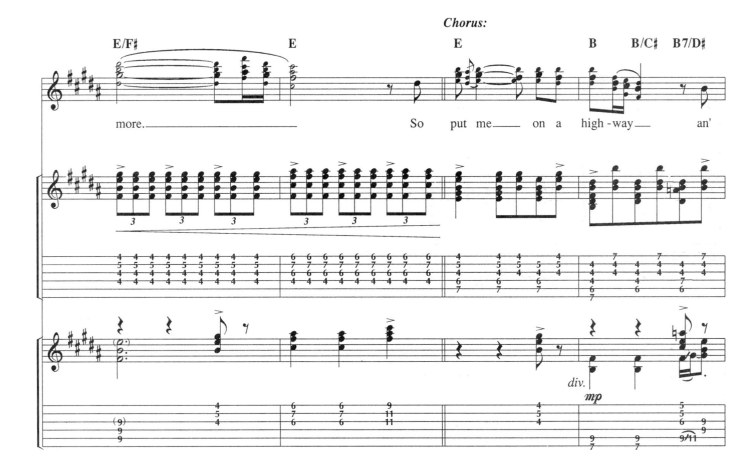

more._____ So put me___ on a high-way___ an'

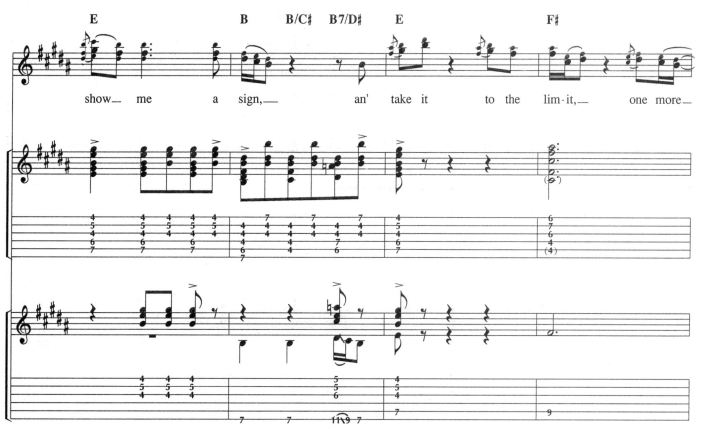

show__ me a sign,__ an' take it to the lim-it,__ one more__

__ time._____ Take it to the lim-it,__

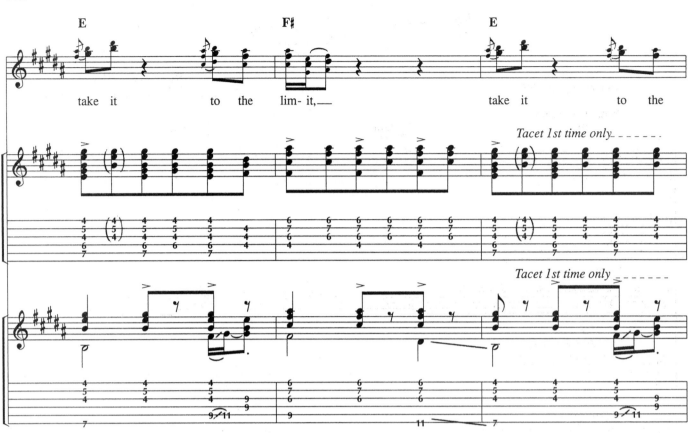

take it   to the lim- it,———   take it   to the

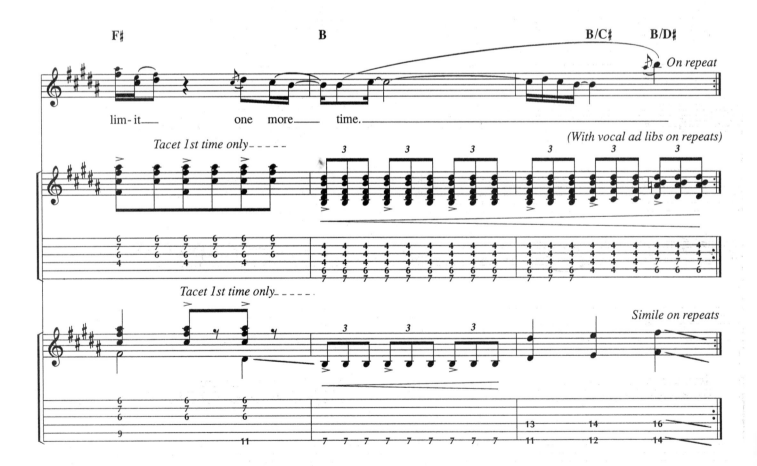

lim- it———   one more——— time.———

Witchy Woman

Words and Music by
BERNIE LEADON and DON HENLEY

Arranged for Guitar 1 as acoustic and/or electric. Doubled by Electric guitar with distortion.

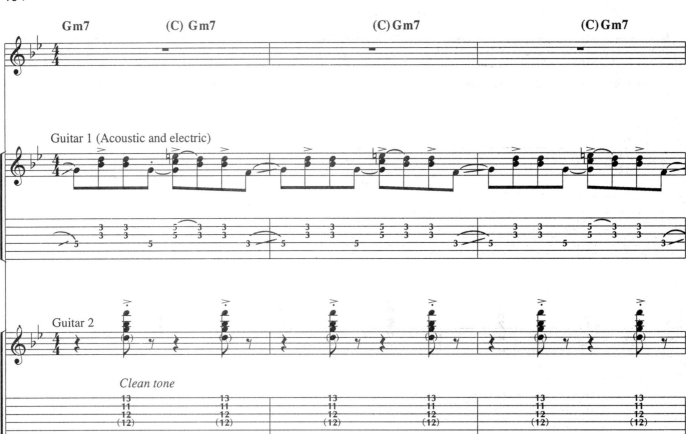

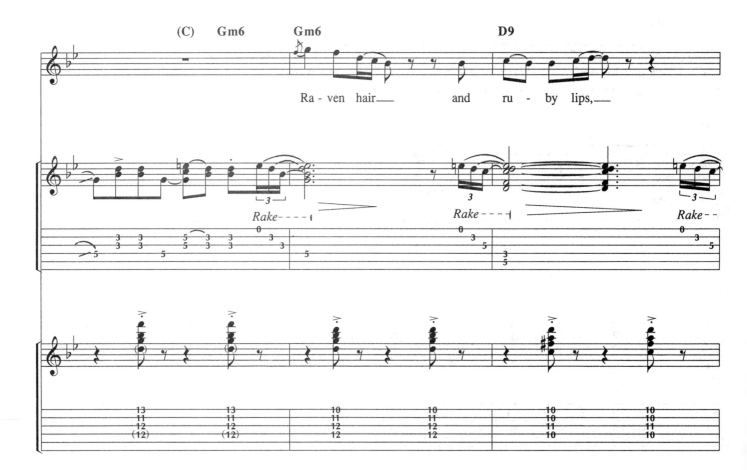

sparks fly from her fin - ger tips.___ Ech - oed voic - es

in___ the night,___ she's a rest - less spir - it on an end - less flight.___

held— me spell-bound in— the night,— danc-ing shad-ows an' fire-light.—

Background Vocals: Oo._____

Cra-zy laugh-ter in an-oth-er room,— an' she drove her-self to mad-ness with a

Oo_____

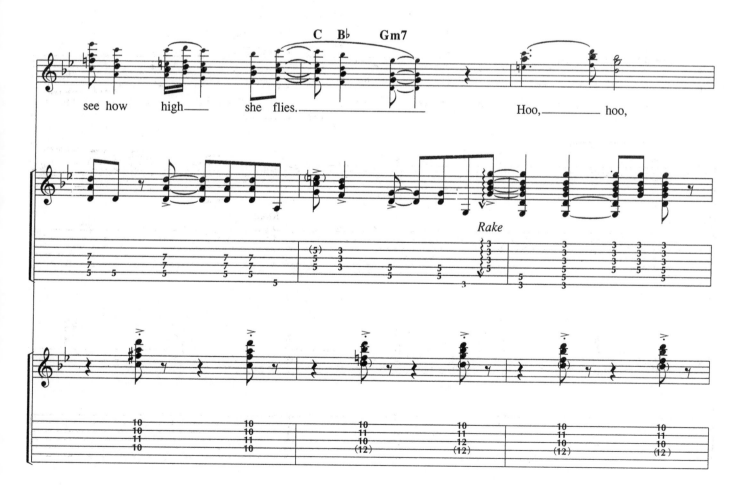

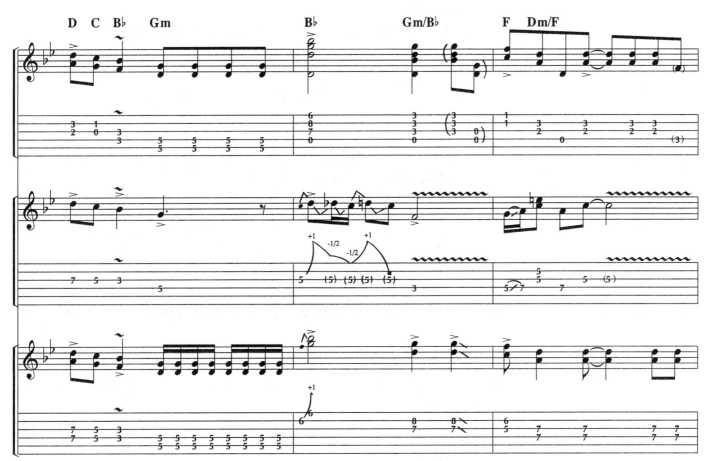

Well, I know

204

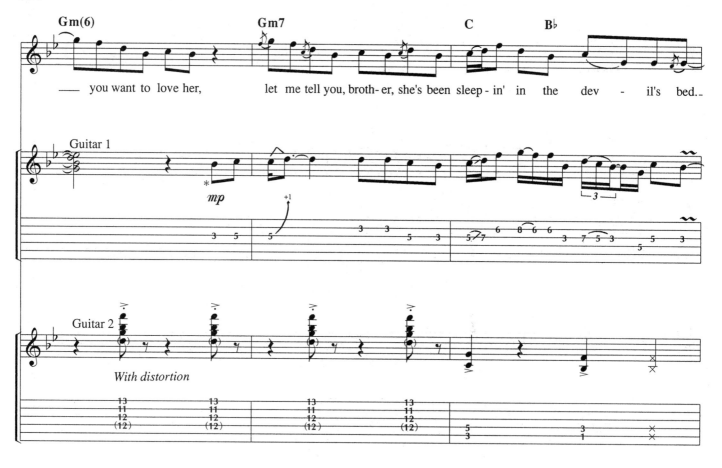

*Two low-mix acoustic guitars arranged here as one.

some-one's un-der-ground,_ she can rock you in the night un-til your skin_ turns red._

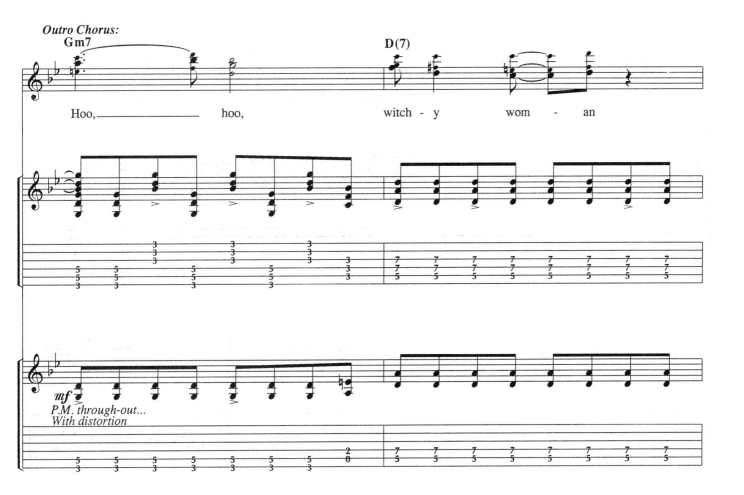

Hoo,_____ hoo, witch-y wom-an

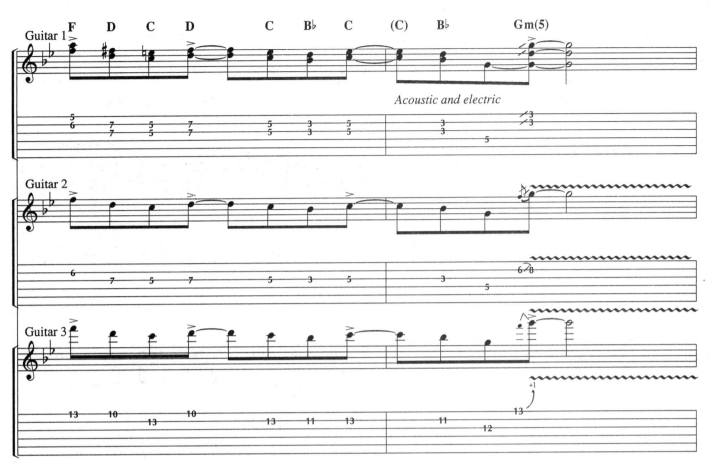